Living Portal Press
An imprint of Emergence Institute
Durango, Colorado, USA

www.livingportalpress.com

Living Portal™, WildCreator™, CosmoSync™, Sequence of Coherence™, and the Involutionary–Evolutionary Flywheel™ are trademarks of Holly Woods, PhD.

ISBN: 978-1-970938-00-5

First Edition: 2026

Printed in the United States of America

Library of Congress Control Number: 2026911012

Table of Contents

Dedication
Author's Note
Preface – Entering the Field of the Living Portal

Part I Remembering the Field

From fragmentation to an animate, coherent universe

Part II The CosmoSync™ Methods

How coherence is restored, stabilized, and embodied

Part III Becoming a Living Portal

From inner coherence to lived, creative participation

"Holly Woods' Radical Wholeness is admirably shamanic in the deepest sense: embodied, transpersonal, intergenerational, and alive to the relational intelligence of fields. It reframes healing not merely as personal repair, but as civic, ecological, and generational service. With the Sequence of Coherence™, coherence markers, and a nuanced understanding of integration, Woods offers a distinctive and much-needed contribution to the next evolution of transformational work."
- **Layman Pascal,** Author of A Universal Learning Process: The Evolution of Meaning and Gurdjieff for a Time-Between-Worlds

"Holly Woods has created something truly powerful: a clear, accessible, and deeply resonant map of fragmentation, coherence, and love as the field through which transformation becomes possible. Her insight that exhaustion often results from living without coherence is both fresh and profoundly useful. This work moved me, and I can already feel its concepts entering my day-to-day life. It belongs in the hands of many more people."
- **Doug Randall,** CEO, Coach, Strategist, TechFounder, Partner, Trium Group

"Holly Woods offers a powerful contribution to a newly emerging paradigm rooted in love and working at the level of frequency. I appreciate how she names the limitations of conventional Parts work and self-improvement, then shows what opens when this work is held from an entirely different perspective. Most importantly, she breaks transformation out of the cult of the individual and returns it to the animate, multidimensional field where it belongs."
- **Joel Monk,** Leadership Coach, Founder, Coaches Rising

"Holly Woods writes from inside the work, not above it. In Radical Wholeness, Parts work is no longer a technique for managing the self, but a serious, embodied, relational, and field-aware path for becoming trustworthy to transformation itself."
-**Darren Gold**, CEO Trium Group

RADICAL WHOLENESS PRIMER

Coherence and Participation In The Living Intelligence of Love

by

Holly Woods, PhD

Part IV Orientation and Integrity

When coherence becomes the ground of life

Part V Coherence in the World

From personal transformation to collective participation

Appendices

Author's Note

This volume is part of a larger body of work published by Living Portal Press, a home for writings that explore the evolution of human consciousness through Love.

The Radical Wholeness Primer is the first book in the *Living Portal Primer Series*. It introduces the conceptual frame, developmental logic, and experiential foundations that ground the CosmoSync™ Methods and the Living Portal Initiation. While the Living Portal includes four major movements—Radical Wholeness, Alignment, WildCreator™, and Cosmic Attunement—this volume focuses on the first and necessary turn of that spiral: the restoration of coherence where fragmentation has shaped identity, perception, and participation in life. That restoration becomes the ground for the broader forms of participation explored in the volumes that follow.

This is not a how-to manual, nor a clinical guide. It is an orienting text. Its purpose is to articulate the ontology, core principles, and lived logic of Radical Wholeness as a field-based approach to healing, coherence, and participation in life. The chapters are best met slowly, as a map and a mirror, rather than as a sequence of techniques to apply.

Radical Wholeness reframes healing not as self-improvement, repair, or regulation alone, but as re-synchronization with a living field of Love. In this work, what are often called "Parts" are approached not merely as psychological subpersonalities or adaptive states, but as sovereign inner Beings: distinct currents of intelligence that reorganize through presence, resonance, and coherent relationship rather than through management or control. As coherence stabilizes, internal opposition softens, energetic waste decreases, and the human system becomes better able to hold complexity without fragmentation.

For readers who prefer to encounter these ideas through lived texture rather than conceptual articulation, *Radical Wholeness: Field Notes* is available as a companion volume. Where this *Primer* offers conceptual architecture, the *Field Notes* offer lived atmosphere and witness. Each can be read independently, and together they form a relational pair.

Appendices are included for readers familiar with Parts-oriented frameworks who wish to understand how Radical Wholeness differs, not primarily in technique, but in ontology. The comparison offered there is not a critique of earlier approaches, but an acknowledgment of the lineage from which this work has emerged and the threshold it seeks to cross.

This book is written for those who sense that healing is not the end of the journey, but the beginning of a deeper participation in life. It is for readers, practitioners, and explorers who are less interested in managing the psyche and more interested in understanding how coherence, creativity, and Love reorganize a human life from the inside out.

Authorship & Language Note

Certain terms used throughout this work—including Sequence of Coherence™, WildCreator™, CosmoSync™, and the Involutionary–Evolutionary Flywheel™—refer to original frameworks and methodologies developed by the author. Trademark symbols are used selectively on first reference to indicate origin; subsequent uses are unmarked in service of readability and flow.

Preface
Entering the Field of the Living Portal

All creation moves through a search for coherence. Radical Wholeness names the first conscious return to that movement within the human form. It begins when a life, long shaped by trauma, adaptation, and cultural trance, begins to feel the living universe again, not as abstraction, but as something intimate, participatory, and already in relation.

This book opens the *Living Portal Primer Series*, a sequence of writings that explores how the CosmoSync Methods restore coherence between psyche, Earth, and Cosmos. CosmoSync is the family of practices that runs through all four pillars of the Living Portal Initiation. It expresses the same field of Love through different modes of practice: Parts work and somatic coherence, purpose alignment, creative embodiment, and cosmic attunement. Underlying these methods is the Sequence of Coherence, the attunement pathway through which fragmentation gives way to stabilized resonance and participatory alignment with life.

These methods emerged through decades of research, lived inquiry, and practice at the threshold where psychology meets physics, ritual meets neuroscience, and the human heart meets a larger field of intelligence.

Radical Wholeness stands within a long lineage of Parts-oriented and consciousness-based approaches. Carl Jung's archetypal psychology revealed the multiplicity of inner life. Hal and Sidra Stone's Voice Dialogue gave those inner figures a voice and a relationship. Richard

Schwartz's Internal Family Systems placed compassion and Self-leadership at the center of healing. Parallel streams in transpersonal psychology, systems work, neuroscience, developmental theory, and ancestral lineages further widened the frame, showing that Parts often carry memory, intelligence, and organization beyond the boundaries of the personal psyche.

Each of these movements marked a genuine advance in how fragmentation could be understood and met.Radical Wholeness stands at a further threshold. Here, the underlying ontology shifts. Psyche is no longer treated primarily as an interior terrain, but as a field phenomenon. Parts are no longer understood solely as psychological subpersonalities or adaptive states, but as living formations of consciousness that carry memory and intelligence across personal, ancestral, karmic, and collective dimensions within an animate universe. Coherence, in this frame, is not something the psyche achieves through management or control. It is a lawful condition of relational alignment within a living reality.

Healing, from this perspective, does not occur primarily through analysis, negotiation, or management. It occurs through re-synchronization with the field of Love that animates life. Once the inner field is restored, the spiral continues through the remaining three harmonics of the Living Portal Initiation:

Alignment, where coherence becomes direction and purpose. **Wild Creator**, where purpose becomes embodied creation. **Cosmic Attunement**, where creation becomes conscious participation in a living universe.

Together, these four movements comprise the Living Portal: a continuum of becoming through which fragmentation gives way to coherence, and personal healing opens into wider participation.

CosmoSync is the methodology—and in a deeper sense, the vibrational technology—that carries these movements. It retains the compassion of Internal Family Systems and the relational ethics of Voice Dialogue, while extending the work into a field-based, multidimensional understanding of coherence. In this frame, Parts are not absorbed into a central Self. They entrain. Distinct waveforms synchronize without losing sovereignty. As coherence stabilizes, internal opposition softens, energetic waste decreases, and the human system becomes more efficient at holding complex patterns without fragmentation.

To engage Radical Wholeness is to participate in Love's own inquiry into how consciousness stabilizes as coherence, how coherence matures into devotion, and how the human being becomes capable of serving as a Living Portal through which the intelligence of life can move more clearly into form.

Chapter 1
Why Radical Wholeness Matters

Radical Wholeness began during a period of my life when I repeatedly entered states of consciousness that took me beyond the familiar boundaries of time, memory, and identity.

Some time ago, after an intense few years of inner work and while still recovering from trauma, dysfunction, and patterns I did not yet fully understand, I found myself moving repeatedly into non-ordinary states of awareness. In those journeys, I would travel beyond the frame of ordinary biography and encounter realities that felt at once otherworldly and unmistakably true. I began perceiving karmic threads moving through my present life, their echoes in childhood, and the repetition of wounds and relational patterns across lifetimes.

What became most significant was the rhythm of moving between them: I would embark on a journey, perceive something beyond the limits of material reality, and then return to ordinary life, carrying an insight I had to decipher. I would come back and recognize the same pattern in my relationships, in my body, in my beliefs, in the emotional and energetic structures that had formed to help me survive. As I moved between liminal awareness and everyday life, I discovered that what appeared in one realm could be traced, tested, and lived in the other.

Over time, this movement revealed something foundational. What we call Parts were not, in my experience, merely psychological fragments or adaptive traits formed within a single lifetime. They appeared as intelligent formations shaped around unresolved rupture, often carrying personal, ancestral, karmic, and transpersonal patterning at once. I came to understand that some Parts were organized not only by what had happened in childhood or in biography, but by fractures in wholeness that had carried across time-space and continued to seek resolution.

This back-and-forth between journey and embodiment became one of the deepest initiatory passages of my life. It changed not only what I understood about trauma and healing, but what I understood about reality itself. The foundations of what would later become the Sequence of Coherence and the Radical Wholeness methods emerged directly from this repeated process of entering, seeing, returning, discerning, and resolving.

The process was not only illuminating. It was heartbreaking. As these patterns revealed themselves, I was not simply gaining insight. I was feeling, often with devastating force, the pain of what had repeated through my own life and beyond it. I would spend hours inside, or in the wake of, a journey overcome by grief. Sometimes I wept with a sorrow so ancient and overwhelming it seemed to belong not only to me, but to the human condition itself.

That grief was both personal and collective. It was personal because I could see, with painful clarity, how trauma, confusion, and fragmentation had shaped my own life, how many wrong turns I had taken, and how often what had not been healed had simply returned in another form. But it was also collective because I could see how endlessly human beings repeat the same suffering across generations, histories, and lifetimes until something in us becomes conscious enough, loving enough, or brave enough to end the pattern at its root. At times, that sorrow felt almost unbearable. It was the grief of seeing how long we wander inside rupture before we remember the way back. Yet what met me there was never condemnation.

Through these experiences, what deepened was not shame but understanding. The Parts I encountered were not indicative of defects or failures. They were intelligent formations shaped around rupture, trying to preserve continuity until they could be brought back into relationship. Beneath the suffering was an intelligence seeking wholeness. Beneath the pattern was an attempt at resolution. And beneath the heartbreak of seeing what I had carried, repeated, and mistaken, there was also the profound relief of discovering that none of it had ever fallen outside the field of a larger divine intelligence.

With each pattern I could finally see, with each wound I could trace, with each Part I could meet and support into coherence, something in me grew lighter. I became freer, more loving toward myself, more trusting of life, and more able to feel that the universe was not empty or indifferent, but participatory and alive.

From this passage of experience, something essential became clear to me: coherence could not be understood only as a state achieved within the material self. What I was encountering was larger than that. Fragmentation was not merely emotional, mental, somatic, energetic, or biographical. It could also be carried across time and space, woven through ancestral inheritance, karmic patterning, and the wider field of being. Coherence, therefore, had to be understood differently. It was not only the integration of the present-day personality, but the restoration of right relationship across the multi-dimensional nature of the Self.

This is the ground from which Radical Wholeness begins. It begins from a different premise than most modern approaches to healing. It does not treat coherence as something we create through force, control, or self-improvement. Radical Wholeness understands coherence as the restoration of what has been divided: in the body, the emotions, the mind, the energetic field, and the deeper transpersonal patterning that may extend across lifetimes. In this sense, coherence is not an achievement. It is the return of what has been separated to a more whole and lawful order.

Much of modern healing work, even when it is compassionate and sophisticated, still operates inside a worldview shaped by separation. It assumes an isolated self, attempting to organize internal experience well enough to function, relate, and perhaps even flourish. That work can bring immense benefit. It can increase self-awareness, soften trauma patterns, deepen emotional range, and reduce inner conflict. I do not dismiss any of that. I have lived inside those lineages for decades, and I know their gifts. But over time, it became clear to me that even the most skillful methods often remain bounded by a frame too small for what a human being is.

A person can become more insight-oriented, more regulated, and more psychologically integrated, and remain subtly organized around separation. A life can become more functional without becoming truly coherent. One can understand the pattern and still not be free of the deeper architecture that keeps the pattern in place.

This is where the distinction between managing and transformation becomes crucial. Much of what passes for healing is, in truth, an improvement in management. Radical Wholeness asks something deeper: what would it mean not simply to manage fragmentation more gracefully, but to restore right relationship where fragmentation once governed the system?

Every human life bears the imprint of separation. Trauma, family systems, culture, and the materialist worldview teach us to experience ourselves as divided. Over time, these divisions cease to be ideas and become structure. Fragmentation shapes the body, the emotions, the mind, the energetic field, and the deeper architecture through which a life is organized.

Fragmentation does not simply mean being wounded, complicated, or emotionally reactive. It means that aspects of the Self and the soul have become cut off from one another, split across layers of experience, or forced into conflict to survive. Some of this fragmentation is personal and biographical. Some of it is familial, ancestral, karmic, or collective.

I came to recognize this fragmentation in myself long before I had a framework for it: the way I could long for intimacy while defending against it, sense a larger destiny while still being organized around fear, or find myself living patterns whose origins could not be explained by this lifetime alone. Fragmentation is the condition in which the human system is no longer moving as an integrated whole, not only within the personality, but across the wider field of one's being.

Many people know this condition without understanding it. They know what it is to be outwardly capable and inwardly overextended. To be thoughtful, accomplished, and sincerely committed to growth, yet still feel that some deeper current of aliveness remains obstructed. They know the fatigue of carrying unresolved tension, the strain of self-management, and the sense that more of life might be available if the system were not working so hard just to hold itself together.

Fragmentation is expensive. It shows up in the nervous system as chronic tension, exhaustion, activation, or shutdown. It appears in attention as narrowing and distraction. It moves through emotional life as reactivity, suppression, or numbness. It shapes relationships through defensiveness, over-accommodation, withdrawal, or mis-attunement. Even a person who is intelligent, capable, and deeply self-aware may still be spending enormous energy simply to remain organized. As long as life-force is bound up in monitoring, bracing, compensating, and internal negotiation, that energy is unavailable for creativity, intimacy, perception, and true participation in life.

Fragmentation is not a moral flaw or private deficiency. It is a costly organizational pattern. And it is also why coherence cannot be restored by insight alone. I do not dismiss insight, regulation, traditional Parts work, psychological integration, somatic healing, or energetic discernment. All of these can be deeply important and support genuine healing. But none of them, by themselves, necessarily transforms the deeper ontology in which the human being is being understood.

These methods may help a person function better within an existing structure without yet transforming the deeper pattern that structure is organized around. They may produce greater flexibility, awareness, or even compassion, while leaving untouched the more fundamental split between Self and world, psyche and field, matter and consciousness.

This was one of the hardest recognitions of my mature work. By the time this became clear to me, I was not looking for a better explanation. I was already living inside very useful conceptual frames and practices. I trusted nuance, knew how to work with story, meaning, adaptation, trauma, and complexity. The maps I had inherited were not wrong, just partial.

The maps we've used have helped us survive and brought extensive healing to much of humanity in profound ways. But these maps could not, on their own, explain what I had come to see so directly: that coherence is not merely an internal state to be achieved, but a relational condition that emerges when the system is no longer organized around separation.

What changed was not my regard for psychological, somatic, energetic, and spiritual approaches to healing, but my recognition that they remained partial when they were not held within a wider understanding of reality. Meaning is not the same as alignment, nor is interpretation the same as participation. One can know a great deal about the origins of a pattern and remain outside the deeper field in which that pattern seeks resolution. There comes a point in serious work when the next movement is not refinement, but reorientation. Not better self-management, but a different relationship to reality itself.

Radical Wholeness arises from that reorientation. Later in this book, I will describe one crucial dimension of fragmentation through the language of Parts: intelligent formations of consciousness that arise to protect continuity around rupture. Some of these formations emerge in response to personal trauma. Some are shaped by ancestral loyalties, karmic residues, or collective patterning. In the CosmoSync Methods, Parts are not treated merely as sub-personalities to be managed or absorbed into a central Self. They are approached as sovereign inner Beings whose restoration into right relationship allows coherence to stabilize without erasing their distinctiveness. They do not disappear into sameness. They entrain. Distinct waveforms synchronize without losing sovereignty.

This is part of what I call the Sequence of Coherence: the natural progression through which what has been fragmented gradually returns to resonance, relationship, and lawful participation in a wider field of wholeness. The sequence is not imposed from outside, nor is it a technique of domination. It reflects what living systems tend to do when interference begins to resolve, and relational integrity is restored. As internal opposition softens, energetic waste decreases. As protective structures no longer need to burn so much energy in vigilance, life-force returns to circulation. The result is not a perfected personality, but a more available human being, one who can hold complexity without collapsing back into fragmentation.

In this sense, Radical Wholeness is not simply another therapeutic modality. It is a form of ontological rehabilitation. It restores human awareness to participation in a living reality that the materialist worldview has taught us to overlook.

For centuries, Western culture has been shaped by a split between subject and object, psyche and world, mind and matter. That split has entered our sciences, our institutions, our methods of healing, and our intimate assumptions about what a human being is. Within that frame, matter is inert, consciousness is secondary, and healing becomes an exercise in repair performed by one isolated self upon another. Radical Wholeness begins elsewhere. It assumes that consciousness is primary, relationship is fundamental, and life is organized through living fields rather than dead mechanisms.

When that ontological shift is felt, not only argued, healing changes; a Part is no longer approached as an intrapsychic problem alone, but as a current of intelligence seeking a restored relationship. Coherence is no longer imagined as a private accomplishment, but as a participatory condition. The human being becomes less a sealed interior and more an organ of relationship within a living cosmos. In this frame, healing is not merely personal relief. It is also civic, ecological, and evolutionary. Presence changes the field. Relationship extends the field. A more coherent human being transmits differently, creates differently, and becomes capable of a different order of participation in life.

There came a point when it was no longer honest for me to think of this work as therapeutic in the usual sense. What was revealed was not simply a better way to heal but a deeper way to participate. I began to see that coherence does not reorganize a life through strategy or control, but through alignment with a larger order already in motion. Creation did not need to be forced. It responded to contact. Openings appeared not as rewards for effort, but as expressions of resonance. My work and my life gradually shifted from management to participation, from standing outside the movement of things to standing inside it.

Radical Wholeness arises in response to a profound distortion of modern life: fragmentation has become so normalized that many people mistake chronic inner division for ordinary functioning. Many are living far below the level of coherence their lives could sustain. Even sophisticated forms of healing can leave untouched the deeper architecture of separation. Life-force is too often spent maintaining defended forms of organization rather than being returned to Love, creation, and presence. And beneath the patterns of rupture, in every human being, there remains a deeper order waiting to be remembered rather than invented or healed. Coherence is what allows a life to stop fighting itself. It returns energy to circulation and makes deeper creativity, intimacy, and truthful participation possible. And it is the first threshold in becoming fully available to one's life.

Chapter 2
The Lineage of Parts Work

I came into this work through lineages that taught me to treat the psyche as multiple, adaptive, and worthy of reverence rather than control.

The recognition that the psyche is multiple rather than singular runs deep in modern depth psychology. Carl Jung's language of complexes and archetypes made it possible to see the inner world as populated rather than unitary, shaped by semi-autonomous figures that move through dreams, symptoms, imagination, and relational life.

Roberto Assagioli's Psychosynthesis extended this multiplicity into a developmental and spiritual arc, naming subpersonalities as expressions of a deeper Self and emphasizing purpose, will, and ethical maturation. I felt the truth of these lineages long before I had language for how fully they would shape my own work.

Later, Hal and Sidra Stone's Voice Dialogue brought a major relational turn. Instead of trying to synthesize the inner world into a single coherent identity, the work invited relationships with inner selves, differentiating awareness from any one state and restoring choice through contact. Richard Schwartz's Internal Family Systems made this relational intelligence widely accessible by offering a clear map of protectors, managers, firefighters, and exiles, anchored in the organizing presence of Self. These approaches changed the moral atmosphere of psychological healing. They dignified adaptation. They treated protection as intelligence rather than as a defect. They helped people stop warring against their own inner lives.

I do not speak of these lineages as an observer. I speak of them as someone formed by them. And they worked and still do. I want to name that plainly, because Radical Wholeness did not arise from a rejection of this lineage. It arose from living inside it long enough to feel both its power and its horizon.

Over the last several decades, additional lineages widened the frame even further. Stanislav and Christina Grof illuminated transpersonal dimensions of psyche, and the way emotionally charged constellations can organize across time, including ancestral and karmic strata. Bert Hellinger's Family Constellations brought systemic loyalties into view, showing how the individual psyche can carry inherited patterns that do not originate in personal biography. Anna Wise's work in Awakened Mind research offered a physiological mirror, showing that expanded awareness and creativity often correlate with synchronization across diverse brainwave patterns. Terri O'Fallon's developmental work clarified that consciousness itself evolves through distinct perspectival capacities, and that inner multiplicity participates in that maturation.

These expansions changed what could be seen. They revealed that Parts are shaped not only by personal history but also by lineage, field dynamics, and developmental timing. Yet even in the most expansive approaches, Parts were still most often treated primarily as aspects of psyche, held within an interior model of healing.

More recently, contemporary post-IFS innovators, including Steve March and other practitioners working at the edge of trauma-informed Parts work, have deepened the practical sophistication of the field. Attachment theory, nervous system education, titration, resourcing, and relational safety have made this work more embodied and more precise. These contributions have been profoundly important. They have helped many people return from overwhelm into dignity, contact, and stable presence, while also clarifying something essential: methods become more effective when they respect the nervous system's thresholds and the body's pace.

These lineages changed the moral atmosphere of my own inner work. They taught me to meet what was conflicted, defended, or fragmented in me without violence.

There was a long season when this work felt like standing inside a beautifully built house—humane, elegant, and remarkably effective. I watched clients soften in ways that still move me to remember. I watched inner wars end, long-exiled energies return, and people regain capacities they thought they had lost forever.

Before I ever felt the limits of these maps, I experienced their beauty firsthand: the way a system softens when protection is met with respect rather than force.

Then a different question began to make itself known, quietly at first, and then with the unmistakable pressure of a new awareness rising. It was not a critique of the map; it was an encounter with its scale. It was precisely because these lineages taught me how to listen so carefully to inner life that I was eventually able to feel where the frame itself was no longer large enough.

Again and again, what wanted to move in people's lives felt larger than a psyche-bound frame could account for. Lineage became known as presence, not as a concept. Time behaved less like a straight line and more like a layered field. Parts arrived not only as inner states but as intelligences with recognizable frequency signatures—carrying personal, ancestral, karmic, and collective material with the same unmistakable fidelity. Through my own profound awareness and reclamation of these lost Parts of my multidimensional Being, I could not unseen this awareness.

This is the threshold where Living Portal Parts Work and the CosmoSync Methods began. In this work, a Part is approached as a sovereign energetic intelligence, a holofractal expression of consciousness, capable of coherence across multiple layers of being. Transformation does not depend primarily on interpretation, integration, or state management. It depends on resonance, on the lawful reorganization that occurs when Parts are met within a living field of Love and coherence. The aim is not to absorb Parts into a central Self as fragments reclaimed, but to restore their sovereignty and entrain them into a harmonic relationship with the whole.

That is the ontological shift Radical Wholeness makes. It doesn't invalidate what came before. It completes a trajectory that the lineage has already been moving toward by naming the level of reality at which the deepest and most precise reorganization is occurring.

Distinctions Between CosmoSync and Conventional Parts Work

CosmoSync stands on the shoulders of IFS, Voice Dialogue, transpersonal psychology, and contemporary trauma-informed refinements. In practice, I draw on the best of these lineages: their dignity, compassion, structural clarity, and respect for protective intelligence. What changes in Radical Wholeness is not the presence of care, but the frame in which coherence is understood.

In many Parts-oriented approaches, whether classical IFS or post-IFS refinements, coherence is treated primarily as a state achieved within the individual system through greater safety, regulation, insight, and integration. This brings real value: it stabilizes the system, reduces reactivity, increases internal trust, and helps the body become a safer place to live.

CosmoSync works with those foundations and then crosses a threshold. Coherence is understood as a graded field condition, a lawful alignment in which information and energy can move through the system without destructive interference. The role of practitioner and participant alike becomes less about managing internal states and more about cultivating the conditions for resonance, so that Parts can return to a harmonic relationship with the whole through entrainment rather than effort. For practitioners, this shift can be seen most clearly across six core dimensions:

Dimension	Conventional IFS / Parts Model	Living Portal™ CosmoSync™ Model
Ontology	Parts are mental sub-personalities inside the psyche.	Parts as energetic intelligences participating in a larger field of consciousness, sovereign nodes of awareness.
Developmental Process	Healing through insight, reframing, and integration.	Through bonding and entrainment, the nervous system learns coherence by resonance.
Time and Lineage	Rooted primarily in personal biography and trauma.	Extends across generations and lifetimes. Parts may complete ancestral or karmic vows.
Agency of Practitioner	Practitioner as interpreter or manager.	Practitioner as field-tuner, cultivating relational coherence through heart-centered presence.

Measurement of Change	Progress is measured by narrative integration and symptom relief.	Transformation tracked through coherence markers: felt stillness, increased regulation, heart-rate variability, and expanded awareness.
Goal of Practice	Self-management and harmony of psyche.	Field coherence is the embodied realization that Self and Cosmos are one living organism.

These distinctions are not theoretical. They change how the work feels in the room, how change unfolds over time, and what kind of stability becomes possible under pressure.

A participant may begin by meeting an anxious Part as a child-self. As contact deepens, the same Part may reveal itself as a lineage-bearing intelligence, carrying an inherited vow or ancestral survival strategy. As coherence increases, it may manifest as a somatic waveform—heat, tremor, contraction—moving through the body at a frequency rather than a story. These layers do not compete. They belong to one another. The work does not require choosing which layer is "true." It requires restoring coherence so that the layers can synchronize without losing sovereignty.

That is why I teach this as architecture. Attractors are not willpower problems; they are the patterns a system returns to under stress. When coherence becomes the attractor, the return is faster, cleaner, and far less costly. Over time, that changes what a life can endure, what it can metabolize, and what it can transmit into its relationships and environments.

In CosmoSync, Parts are not treated as fragments to be harmonized into a single psychological center. They are approached as distinct notes within a larger chord of being. Healing becomes the restoration of resonance among intelligences within the larger field of Self, and coherence becomes the condition that allows that chord to hold across time.

This also reframes development. Each Part is not simply unburdened. It matures. It grows into its gift. It becomes capable of service and contribution. That maturation changes the internal economy of life-force. As protective strategies soften, energy returns to circulation. Creativity becomes more available. Timing sharpens. Relational fields change because the system is no longer spending itself on internal opposition.

The fuller comparative map is offered in Appendices A and B. For now, the essential point is simpler: Radical Wholeness carries forward the compassion and relational intelligence of the Parts lineage while shifting its ontology from psyche-bound healing to field-based coherence. This is the threshold where the Living Portal begins.

From the Inside of Radical Wholeness: When the Map Was No Longer Big Enough

I am here because of the lineage I come from. They shaped my perception, gave me language for multiplicity and for reverence toward protection, and taught me to meet my inner world without violence.

By the time Living Portal and CosmoSync began to take form, I was not searching for a new model. I was living inside the models that already existed, refining them through practice, letting them change me and the lives of the people I served.

What shifted was not my respect for the lineage. What shifted was my allegiance to the size of its frame.

There comes a point in any mature discipline when the question changes. It stops being, "How do we do this well?" and becomes, "What reality is this actually happening in?" That question reorganized my work. Parts stopped behaving like interior psychological content and began revealing themselves as sovereign intelligences participating in a living field of time, lineage, and nonlocal coherence.

I did not leave the old maps behind. I carried them with me into the larger territory they were already pointing toward.

Chapter 3
The Limits of the Psychological Paradigm

The modern psychological frame rests on a few assumptions so familiar that we rarely pause to examine them. Consciousness is treated as something the brain produces. Healing is understood as the result of insight, integration, and behavioral change. Time is assumed to move in a straight line, with past wounds causing present symptoms that can be repaired through future choice.

These assumptions have given us many useful maps. They have helped people make meaning of suffering, restore function, and reclaim lost capacities. I know those maps from the inside. I built much of my early work within them, trusted their elegance, and witnessed how much genuine healing they could make possible. And there came a point when I could no longer ignore a particular kind of fatigue that kept appearing in myself and in people who were, by every psychological measure, doing very well.

This was not a collapse or depletion in any simple sense. It was more nuanced and structural: a persistent friction in the system, as though energy were being spent simply to maintain internal organization. Depletion is a lack of energy. What I was seeing was different. Energy was present, but bound up in holding, monitoring, and negotiating inside the Self.

By the time I could see this clearly, I had been on the path long enough to know how much coherence is possible through insight, relational work, and integration. I had watched people reorganize in profound ways. and had done so myself. The maps were elegant and functional. And still, there was a growing sense that something more fundamental was being asked—not a better arrangement of the psyche, but a different relationship to the field in which the psyche lives.

What I was noticing did not feel like a failure of healing. It felt like standing at the edge of a very refined architecture and realizing that the architecture itself was built inside a larger order it did not fully account for.

Within the psychological paradigm, strain of this kind is often interpreted as pathology; fragmentation becomes something to fix. The task becomes rearranging the inner system until harmony prevails. But what if fragmentation is not a malfunction so much as an interference pattern within a wider waveform of consciousness? What if much of what we call vigilance or defense is, at root, care— intelligent organization stemming from conditions of threat or uncertainty?

Protection is not a mistake. It is an intelligent constraint, a lawful adaptation that emerges under conditions of threat or uncertainty. The difficulty arises when that constraint outlives the conditions that necessitated it, and the system continues to expend energy maintaining a boundary that no longer matches its environment.

For many years, I trusted meaning completely. I built my work around listening for story, history, adaptation, and intent. What began to change was not my respect for interpretation, but my certainty that interpretation was the same thing as coherence. I started to see, again and again, that a life could be exquisitely understood and still be oriented from a frame that placed it just slightly outside the larger order it belonged to.

The question was no longer whether the story made sense. The question was whether the system itself was standing inside the field that was already coherent.

This is where Radical Wholeness begins to diverge from a purely psychological approach. It treats the psyche not only as a narrative system, but as an energetic topology within a living field. The guiding movement shifts from causal repair to field entrainment, from management to resonance. The central question is no longer only "What happened to me?" but "How has my system fallen out of rhythm with the field of life, and how might it return to coherence within it?"

In this orientation, the healing space becomes less like a site of diagnosis and more like a tuning chamber. Insight remains useful, but it is not sufficient. What reorganizes a system at depth is not explanation alone, but resonance.

The body tells this story more honestly than language does. Shoulders held a few centimeters too high. A jaw that never quite rests. Breath shortened, not from fear, but from readiness that never stands down. Attention scanning for what might require a response. When coherence returns, nothing dramatic needs to happen. The shoulders lower. The jaw releases. Breath finds its own rhythm. The system stops bracing and begins to organize from within.

This is the threshold where the CosmoSync Methods and the Sequence of Coherence begin their real work: not at the level of cognition, but at the level of how the system is oriented inside the field of life. For me, this crossing required a different posture rather than a new technique. I began to realize that what was reorganizing people was not the elegance of my questions or the sophistication of my models, but the degree to which the work was held within a coherent field of relationships. The center of gravity shifted from explanation to participation. I was no longer primarily helping people understand their lives. I was learning how to stand with them inside a larger order that could remember itself through us.

From here, the role of the facilitator changes. We stop acting mainly as analysts of meaning and become stewards of coherence. The intelligence that reorganizes a human being is not primarily cognitive. It is harmonic. It is a remembering of the body-soul's rightful pitch within the larger music of life.

Philosophical and Scientific Context for a Paradigm Shift

Across many disciplines, a related turn is quietly underway. Thinkers such as Iain McGilchrist, Antonio Damasio, and Francisco Varela have each challenged strictly mechanistic accounts of mind in different ways. McGilchrist has shown how right-hemisphere modes of perception sustain contextual, embodied, and relational contact with a living world, while left-hemisphere dominance tends toward abstraction and control. Damasio's work has helped restore the inseparability of mind, body, and feeling. Varela's enactive model reframes cognition as arising through dynamic coupling with the environment rather than within an isolated skull.

Much contemporary therapeutic work quite rightly emphasizes regulation. Regulation restores safety, range, and basic functional stability to stressed systems. It helps people come back from overwhelm, freeze, and collapse. But regulation works within a given architecture. It improves how a system runs. It does not, by itself, change what the system is organized around.

When fatigue or friction persists in otherwise highly skilled, self-aware, and resourced people, the issue is often not a lack of technique. It is a signal that a deeper reorganization is being asked for.

In quantum biology and systems theory, coherence refers to the capacity of complex systems to maintain alignment in the presence of disturbance. It does not mean the absence of noise. It means that information can move through the system without being scattered into interference. In living systems, this kind of organization is metabolically efficient. Less energy is wasted in internal opposition. More becomes available for perception, adaptation, and creativity.

From this perspective, exhaustion often marks a system expending energy to maintain constraints that no longer fit its environment. Coherence arises as those constraints relax and the system returns to a more economical, truthful organization.

Seen this way, the mechanistic psyche is not wrong, just partial. It reflects an Industrial Age epistemology built on separation, control, and optimization. Those maps helped us survive. They cannot, by themselves, reveal what lies beyond repair: the capacity to live as coherence rather than manage against fragmentation.

Radical Wholeness resonates with what systems philosopher Daniel Schmachtenberger calls the Third Attractor, one that neither collapses into chaos nor tightens into control but reorganizes around relational coherence. In this frame, the practitioner does not fix trauma so much as cultivate the conditions for resonance to return. When coherence stabilizes, the system begins to reorganize according to its deeper pattern of wholeness. Physicist David Bohm might describe this as the implicate order returning to expression, hidden coherence unfolding again into lived form.

Nothing essential is lost in this process. Protective intelligence is not dismantled, but reassigned. Energy once bound in monitoring, bracing, and internal negotiation becomes available for repair, creativity, and connection. The system does not become less intelligent, just less costly. The effort required to maintain earlier constraints and to participate in life is diminished or resolved.

To practice within the Living Portal is to participate in this larger remembering. Healing becomes a mutual act between human and world, each attuning the other back into rhythm. As the Sequence of Coherence unfolds, Parts—understood here as sovereign inner Beings—reorganize not through force or persuasion, but through their natural capacity to entrain with a wider field of coherence.

Often, the system recognizes this readiness before the mind has language for it. Exhaustion arrives as information, not as inadequacy. The system loosens its grip before the story of permission is fully formed. In that opening, nothing needs to be forced. Coherence does not require trust in advance; it generates trust as it stabilizes.

From the Inside of Radical Wholeness: When Insight Was No Longer Enough

I had long since made peace with complexity. What I had not yet understood was how exhausting it is to remain organized inside a frame that has become too small for one's lived reality.

What began to reveal itself was a more subtle limit: not the limit of understanding, but the limit of a paradigm that still placed coherence inside the psyche rather than in the field that psyche inhabits.

It became clear that even the most sophisticated psychological models remain, at their core, models of optimization. They help a system function better within a given architecture. They do not, by themselves, question what that architecture is organized around.

The exhaustion I kept seeing in high-functioning, deeply resourced people—including myself at times—was not a failure of skill or insight. It was the cost of maintaining an orientation that had outlived its cosmology.

What changed my work was not abandoning meaning but realizing that meaning is not the same as alignment. That interpretation is not the same as participation. That coherence is not produced by understanding but revealed when a system is no longer organized around separation.

At this point in my work, I understood that the next step was not about refinement of existing maps, but a reorientation. None of this indicated a failure or a crisis, but an invitation to explore beyond our knowing of reality.

Chapter 4
The Ontological Shift From Fragmentation to Animacy

To move from psychological integration to Radical Wholeness requires more than a new method. It requires a different ontology, one in which Love is recognized not as an emotion or an ethic, but as a structuring principle of reality itself.

The mechanistic worldview assumes inert matter animated by isolated minds. Within that frame, healing is understood as repair: reorganizing the parts, restoring function, and helping the system operate with greater stability and control. The animate worldview begins somewhere else entirely. It recognizes that matter is not inert, that consciousness is not merely produced by form but expressed through it, and that every living system participates in a wider field of relational intelligence.

I did not arrive here through philosophy alone, but through repeated encounters in which life stopped appearing as an inert backdrop and began to reveal itself as responsive, relational, and already in communication. What changed was not merely what I believed but what reality itself began to feel like. The world no longer appeared to be a neutral setting in which healing occurred. It began to feel more like a living field within which healing, perception, and participation were already taking place.

Once this becomes felt rather than merely argued, the psyche can no longer be understood as a sealed interior. It reveals itself as an organ of relationship. A Part is no longer approached simply as an intrapsychic artifact, a symptom cluster, or a defensive adaptation located inside an isolated self. It is encountered as a current of intelligence carrying tone, history, and purpose within a wider field of life. In the Living Portal, these Parts are engaged as sovereign inner Beings. Their reorganization does not occur through cognitive rearrangement alone, but through the Sequence of Coherence, as the relational field is restored and resonance stabilizes.

This shift also changes what we mean by Love. Here, Love is not sentiment, virtue, or intention. It is a capacity carried by a structure. When a system is fragmented, that capacity is unstable and easily exhausted. Love may still be felt, desired, or sincerely intended, but it cannot circulate reliably because the architecture that would carry it is divided against itself. When coherence stabilizes, Love becomes more durable, not because anyone is trying harder, but because the conditions that allow it to move without distortion have been restored.

From here, development must also be understood differently. The psyche does not heal in straight lines. In an animate universe, processes unfold through spirals: recurring arcs of return, refinement, and reorganization visible across scales. We see this logic of patterned return in the body, in the rhythms of the nervous system, in cycles of growth and decay, and in how perception develops over time. Radical Wholeness does not collapse Parts into a single center. It invites them back into the larger spiral through which life reorders itself into coherence.

I did not come to this through a romantic attachment to nonlinearity. I came to it because, over time, it became impossible not to notice that growth itself moves by re-encounter rather than erasure. What once looked like repetition began to reveal itself as refinement, as a widening arc that can only be recognized from a different altitude. The spiral stopped feeling like a metaphor and began to reveal itself as a lawful pattern of life, one that does not discard what has been, but continuously repositions it within a larger coherence.

This changes the stance of the practitioner and participant alike. We no longer handle or process Parts as if they were objects. We meet them. Each carries a rhythm, an image, a signature, a way of holding experience that has its own integrity. When met with presence rather than force, these signatures begin to entrain with the organism's wider field, remembering the harmony that has always been implicit. The practitioner follows the rhythm of the Sequence of Coherence, supporting the Part's return to relational safety and resonance rather than directing its outcome.

The relief that follows is not an emotional uplift or a spiritual peak. It is structural. It is the quiet cessation of an internal labor that was never meant to be permanent. The system spends less energy holding itself together and more energy simply being itself.

What I recognized was not a new feeling state, but a change in orientation. The human system no longer had to be managed toward coherence. It was standing inside it. Life did not become simpler, but it became more precisely encountered. I did not solely experience increased regulation or greater comfort, but alignment: the sense that less effort was required, not because less was being asked, but because the asking and the responding were finally happening within the same relational field.

This is the animate paradigm at the heart of the Living Portal Initiation. Psyche, body, Earth, and cosmos are not separate domains. They are expressions of one living continuum of Love. The central question shifts from "How do I fix myself?" to "How do I participate in the field that is already coherent?"

From this perspective, fragmentation can also be understood differently. It is not only damage or deficiency. It can also be a form of specialization under conditions of rupture. Each Part carries a strand of the larger design, awaiting remembrance and re-entry into the weave. Healing becomes communion rather than repair. It is the moment coherence remembers itself through a human life.

This reorganization does not first announce itself through dramatic changes in circumstance. It is felt initially as a quieter center of gravity within the system, a reduction in internal friction, a return of attention to its natural coherence. Only from this stability does life begin to respond differently, not as reward, but as resonance finding its own pathways.

Animate Paradigm Context and Scholarship

The animate worldview is not new. It appears in many of the oldest human cosmologies, from Indigenous traditions that understand the world as alive and communicative, to the *anima mundi* of Renaissance thought, to Teilhard de Chardin's vision of the noosphere as an evolving field of consciousness. Across these very different lineages runs a shared recognition: mind and matter are not separate substances, but different expressions of one living reality.

Several contemporary thinkers and fields of inquiry lend partial support to this shift in perception. Iain McGilchrist's work on hemispheric asymmetry has helped clarify how the right hemisphere is specialized for context, relationship, embodied presence, and living wholes, while the left excels at abstraction, manipulation, and control.

Modern culture's overreliance on left-hemisphere modes of knowing mirrors a deeper civilizational split between human beings and the living world. Among other things, Radical Wholeness can be understood as a neurological and ontological reconciliation, a return to perception that can once again register life as alive.

Ecotheologian Thomas Berry described this civilizational transition as the Great Work: the movement from a technological civilization toward a communion of subjects. Within the Living Portal, this is not treated merely as an idea to endorse, but as an experience to inhabit. The psyche stops functioning solely as an isolated narrative and begins to operate more like a sensorium of Earth–Cosmos dialogue. What once seemed like private interiority reveals itself as participation in a much larger relational field.

As coherence stabilizes, life often begins to meet the system differently. Time becomes more opportunistic. Interactions carry less friction. Resources appear when we are ready for them. This is not because coherence is a strategy for getting what we want, but because a system no longer divided against itself can participate more accurately in the larger relational field. Synchronicity is not a reward, but an indicator of a restored dialogue between inner and outer worlds.

Across physics, biology, and systems theory, coherence is linked with reduced internal interference, greater efficiency, and more reliable coordination. When internal opposition resolves, energy is no longer spent on constraint, and the system begins to move as a more unified whole. In the language of the CosmoSync Methods, this is coherence in action: not a mystical overlay imposed on experience, but the lawful reorganization that becomes possible when fragmentation no longer governs the field.

From here, the human system relinquishes its managerial role of experience and becomes a tuning instrument within a larger field of resonance. Each heartbeat, each breath, each moment of presence participates in a larger rhythm of creation. When Love is understood as the field itself, coherence is no longer a personal accomplishment. It becomes a way life remembers itself through form.

From the Inside of Radical Wholeness: When the World Became a Relationship

For most of my adult life, I was working at the level of refinement rather than repair. I had spent decades inside the great lineages, listening, integrating, apprenticing myself to the deep architectures of psyche, energy, and meaning. By the time this work began to take shape, I was not looking for healing in the ordinary sense. I was looking for the place where even the most sophisticated maps give way to lived alignment.

I noticed that my understanding of Parts and my relationship to the world itself had changed. Life no longer felt like a backdrop and began to feel relational. Patterns no longer appeared as isolated psychological events but instead arrived as communications within a living field. What I had once treated as internal material alone began to reveal its participation in something larger: lineage, timing, environment, intelligence, and the quiet reciprocity between inner and outer life.

It happened too consistently, and with too much precision, to be reduced to a metaphor. A Part did not need to be convinced. A history did not need to be argued with, and a pattern did not need to be overpowered. What was required was the restoration of conditions under which circulation could resume. When that happened, change was not dramatic so much as inevitable.

This is where my understanding of healing shifted permanently: away from technique and toward ecology, away from control and toward coherence, away from fixing and toward restoring lawful movement in a living field. The heart revealed itself not as a symbol, but as an oscillator. The field revealed itself not as an abstraction, but as the medium in which real reorganization takes place. Parts revealed themselves not as problems to solve, but as concentrated carriers of life-force waiting for circulation to become possible again.

This work exists because there is a profound difference between managing energy and participating in its return to flow. One creates temporary order; the other restores a living one. CosmoSync works not because it applies the correct intervention from the outside, but because it learns to stop interrupting the innate intelligence of a broader field, trying to reclaim coherence.

Radical Wholeness did not emerge from a need to be repaired. It emerged from reaching the upper edge of what psychological and spiritual maps could carry, and discovering that what remained was not another method, but a different belonging to a universe that was never an object to be mastered, only a living order to be joined.

Chapter 5
The Living Portal
CosmoSync Methods

CosmoSync names the integrated methodology by which the Four Pillars of the Living Portal Initiation—Radical Wholeness, Soul Alignment, WildCreator, and Cosmic Attunement—function as one harmonic system. It is both a developmental path and an energetic technology: a living sequence through which Love organizes itself in human form.

CosmoSync is not a single protocol. It is a family of methods that recur across the four pillars in different octaves. In Radical Wholeness, it appears as Parts work and trauma alchemy that restores internal coherence and returns life-force to circulation. In Soul Alignment, it becomes purpose work and belief-system transmutation grounded in somatic intelligence, developmental psychology, and neuroscience. In WildCreator, it takes form as quantum fieldwork, creativity, and prototyping practices that awaken sourced creation. In Cosmic Attunement, it extends into nature-based and transpersonal practices that stabilize the relationship with Earth and Cosmos as a living context.

I did not set out to "create a method." I was sitting with people, week after week, year after year, noticing what remained reliable even when I changed everything else. Particular moments in a session were illuminating, certain sequences stabilized the system, and specific kinds of inquiry opened the same doors, even when the person, the story, and the circumstances were entirely different.

There were times I tried to move more quickly than the sequence allowed, thinking insight alone would be enough, or assuming that once a Part was visible, it was ready to change. Repeatedly, the system taught me otherwise. When I respected the order in which trust, contact, revelation, and reorganization unfolded, coherence deepened. When I rushed it, something essential closed. Over time, I began to understand that the sequence was not mine to impose. It was something life itself seemed to prefer. I came to think of this as moving at the "Speed of Love," because only at that pace could the deeper intelligence of the system return without distortion.

What eventually became CosmoSync did not begin as an innovation. It emerged through years of listening, testing, and staying faithful to what consistently reorganized a human system when the field was genuinely met. I was not designing a framework so much as recognizing a pattern that kept revealing itself, until it became clear that something larger was organizing the work.

Over time, the same movements revealed themselves across wildly different lives—not as technique, but as lawful choreography. I began to recognize that Love has its own sequencing: its own intelligence about when contact is possible, when truth can be metabolized, when a Part can be held without distortion, when creation can safely come online.

Together, these methods move through what I call the Involutionary–Evolutionary Flywheel, a repeating spiral in which the system first turns inward to reclaim what has been split or exiled and then turns outward again to express that recovered coherence as creativity, contribution, and new form. It names the rhythm I kept witnessing: descent into density, return to coherence, and re-emergence into life. Through this sequence, participants move from fragmentation into coherence, and from coherence into emergent creation rooted in Love.

The Three Premises

CosmoSync is built on three premises that name the basic physics of coherence:

1. **The Universe is Coherent.** Everything, including trauma, participates in lawful patterning.

2. **Human Systems Mirror Cosmic Systems.** The microcosm of the body-mind reproduces the macro-patterns of the cosmos.

3. **Resonance Restores Order.** When resonance is restored, information flows more cleanly, and life reorganizes.

These premises were not adopted as beliefs; they became obvious through encounter. The longer I worked, the harder it became to ignore how consistently even the densest experiences—trauma, rupture, ancestral inheritance, karmic vow—still moved according to lawful patterns, as if nothing had ever been outside coherence, only temporarily occluded from it. I watched human systems mirror cosmic systems with a precision that was difficult to dismiss: spirals, phase shifts, descent, and return, revealing themselves across different lives. And I learned, in hundreds of unremarkable moments, that the turning point was rarely force or insight. It was resonance: the moment a system was met in a way it could finally recognize, and order returned as if it had been waiting all along.

Within this framework, Parts Work becomes less a negotiation among internal positions and more a process of field synchronization. Each Part possesses a distinct frequency signature, a density of stored emotion, belief, and lineage imprint, that begins to re-enter harmony when met by coherent presence.

In later stages of Radical Wholeness, participants are guided to build an inner coherence chamber—a Mind Palace or inner sanctuary—so the system has a stable architecture in which Parts can relate, reorganize, and collaborate without overwhelm. Integration is not an act of fixing. It is entrainment to Love through the Sequence of Coherence.

The Six A's of Radical Wholeness

Six phases form the practical arc of the CosmoSync process within the Radical Wholeness pillar:

Acknowledge – Accept – Allow – Appreciate – Aspire – Alchemize.

These phases spiral through time, deepening trust between Self and Part, and mirroring the Involutionary–Evolutionary Flywheel: descent into density (Acknowledge to Allow) and ascent into radiance (Appreciate to Alchemize). Each phase is psychological, somatic, and energetic at once. It is how Love translates into matter without coercion.

The Six A's unfold in alignment with the Sequence of Coherence. They move at the pace the system can safely hold. They are not instructions to "do it right." They are landmarks that help practitioners and participants recognize what the system is ready for and what it is not.

The Six A's are not arbitrary stages. They reflect a recurring logic visible across coherent systems: inward stabilization, relational deepening, and outward reorganization.

CosmoSync also mirrors the geometric architecture of coherent systems. Across organisms and the cosmos, growth tends to move through spiraling sequences—toroidal flows, phi ratios, logarithmic expansions. Marshall Lefferts describes these as cohering geometries in cosmometry: patterns by which complex systems stabilize, deepen, and then expand. The Six A's follow a similar rhythm. Each turn deepens inward, stabilizes the center, and then arcs outward into increased complexity and expression. Healing is not linear progress but spiral entrainment, the return to the universal pattern through which all coherent systems evolve.

Phase	Neurobiological State	Energetic Movement
Acknowledge	Prefrontal integration recognizes the Part	Waveform identified as a distinct frequency
Accept	Vagal toning increases, threat response drops	Amplitude stabilizes within the heart field
Allow	Interoceptive awareness opens the insula	Oscillation between density and light begins
Appreciate	Oxytocin and trust rise	Frequency enters phase alignment
Aspire	Meaning-based motivation activates dopaminergic pathways	Coherence extends beyond the skin field
Alchemize	Gamma synchrony may increase as heart-brain coordination deepens	A new standing pattern emerges as coherence stabilizes

In simple terms, the process begins by noticing the Part, relaxing enough to remain in contact, allowing it to speak, appreciating its original role, envisioning new possibilities, and then supporting the transformation of the energy it carries through a new form of relationship.

Beyond Radical Wholeness: The Spiral Across the Four Pillars

Radical Wholeness is the first turning of the Living Portal spiral. It restores coherence to the Self-system and reclaims the lost currency of life-force. The journey toward becoming a Living Portal continues through three additional movements—Soul Alignment, WildCreator, and Cosmic Attunement—each introducing further stages of the same evolutionary current.

Where Radical Wholeness restores coherence, Soul Alignment gives that coherence direction. Where Soul Alignment establishes a coherent trajectory, WildCreator liberates the creative force that coherence makes safe. Where WildCreator awakens sourced creation, Cosmic Attunement situates that creation within Earth and Cosmos as a living context.

These movements form a continuum of A's, progressive attunements of the same intelligence across different octaves of development:

Pillar	Theme	Core A's
I. Radical Wholeness	Restoration of the inner field	Acknowledge, Accept, Allow, Appreciate, Aspire, Alchemize
II. Alignment	Optimization of coherence	Alchemize II, Applaud, Amplify
III. WildCreator™	Liberation of creative force	Animate, Audacity, Accelerate
IV. Cosmic Attunement	Integration with the living universe	Announce, Adapt, Affinities / Allies

Together, these Four Pillars trace the Sequence of Coherence, the same spiral seen in nature's growth patterns, the Involutionary–Evolutionary Flywheel, and the sacred geometries of creation. Each

"A" is not just an action, but an attunement, a resonant octave in the unfolding of wholeness.

It took time for me to trust that these were not separate domains I was stitching together. I watched people move through these phases often enough to recognize the pattern before I had language for it. When I stopped treating the pillars as modules and began relating to them as a single harmonic system, the Living Portal clarified itself. The sequence was not conceptual. It was musical. Each pillar revealed itself as an overtone of the one note.

Somatic and Energetic Sequencing

CosmoSync operates through the body as an instrument. Grounding and vagal regulation establish safety. Capacity expands through breath, micro-movement, and attention. Only then is deeper contact made with the Part, because a system cannot entrain with what it cannot tolerate.

When the field coheres, the body often signals completion through warmth, trembling, tears, or stillness. These are not simply "releases." They are phase shifts—tangible signatures of reorganization that correspond with the Sequence of Coherence and help determine when a Part is ready for deeper contact, and when it needs more time, structure, or pacing.

When Love arises from coherence rather than effort, it is often felt as a settled warmth rather than intensity. The chest softens. Breath moves without management. Attention stops scanning for threat or approval. The body rests in contact. This is not the relief of collapse, nor the charge of attachment, but the felt sense of a system no longer organized around protection.

Polyvagal and HeartMath as Measurement

Research associated with Stephen Porges' polyvagal theory, along with work from the HeartMath Institute on heart-brain coherence, suggests that when heart and brain rhythms enter a more ordered relationship, autonomic function can reorganize and heart-rhythm patterns may become more coherent, with measurable effects on attention, emotional stability, and relational presence.

From within the CosmoSync frame, these findings are not the cause of coherence. They are its signatures. Physiology does not explain Love. It registers what becomes possible when a system is no longer divided against itself. The instruments confirm what the relational field is already doing.

The Relational Field

As coherence stabilizes, Love no longer remains confined to the interior or even to human relationships alone. The same capacity that allows Parts to relate without protection begins to shape how the organism meets the world. Attention and responsiveness become less defensive or reactive and more precise. This is not moral improvement. It is functional evolution: a system that no longer expends energy on internal opposition can participate in larger fields with less distortion.

Because the field is alive, everything in the room participates. Practitioners sometimes notice shifts in sound, temperature, or sensory awareness. Symbols arise. Energy shifts. Synchronicities punctuate or arise adjacent to a session. Within this frame, these are not trophies or proofs. They are entrainment phenomena—signs that the wider field is re-patterning in relationship with a human system returning to coherence.

Field Theory and Collective Coherence

Physicist David Bohm's concept of the implicate order offers a language for this mutual co-arising: part and whole fold into each other continuously. Rupert Sheldrake's hypothesis of morphic resonance offers a provocative analogy: when one system stabilizes a pattern, it can become easier for similar systems to access that pattern.

Whether or not one accepts Sheldrake's claims as literal science, the practical observation remains: coherence is not private. When a nervous system stabilizes, relational dynamics change. When a relational dynamic changes, the group field changes. When the group field changes, new options become thinkable and speakable. Coherence, in circulation, becomes a form of responsibility.

This process becomes even more palpable once participants have an inner structure, such as a Mind Palace, that anchors and amplifies relational coherence. A stable inner landscape allows Parts to be perceived without overwhelm and gives the system a consistent way to return to orientation under pressure.

The Dignity of the Part

Every Part has a positive intent and a deeper purpose. A critical inner voice may guard a lineage of grief. An anxious protector may carry the evolutionary impulse to adapt. When greeted with reverence rather than correction, each Part begins to reveal its deeper function and naturally reorganizes toward service within the whole.

This emergence is consistent with Stanislav Grof's observation that inner guidance becomes more coherent as the organism experiences enough safety to metabolize what was previously defended. Under conditions of attunement, even highly armored Parts begin to show their deeper intelligence.

Honoring a Part's dignity creates a secure attachment not only within the psyche but within the field itself. It mirrors early bonding dynamics, yet it extends beyond them: as each Part feels safely held, it graduates from defense to contribution. As coherence deepens, Parts reveal themselves as sovereign inner Beings—not through force, but through acknowledgment, pacing, and relational integrity. Once recognized, their gifts come forward with surprising inevitability.

Integration as Re-patterning

In IFS, unburdening removes pain from Parts. In CosmoSync, coherence re-patterns the field so that a Part's energy can circulate as creative power. What once blocked vitality now becomes a generator of it. The practitioner does not discard Parts, but redeems their frequency, folding them back into the organism's evolving symphony.

This is also how Love becomes sustainable. Many people are not failing at Love. They are working too hard at it. When a system is fragmented, Love must be carried by effort, vigilance, and negotiation. Conflict and collapse often reflect structural strain: a system attempting to sustain connection without the coherence required to hold it with ease.

Each re-patterning is a micro-ecological event. The individual becomes a self-healing biosphere. Energy once used for containment returns to creativity, supporting not only personal expression but also relational and civic resilience. A coherent system makes fewer distorted demands on its surroundings. It projects less, grasps less, consumes less, and escalates less blindly. Love, carried by coherence, becomes responsibility rather than performance.

Integration also includes the intentional creation of inner architecture: a Mind Palace or comparable coherence structure in which sovereign inner Beings can reside, reorganize, and collaborate. Not just symbolic, this inner architecture functions as a coherence chamber, stabilizing previously fragmented capacities into new patterns of being.

Gaston Bachelard wrote in *The Poetics of Space* that interior environments shape the psyche's capacity to organize meaning and experience. An intentionally constructed inner architecture applies this insight inwardly by shaping the conditions of the inner environment. A coherent inner architecture strengthens orientation, stability, and the system's capacity to evolve.

In times like ours, coherence is not a private luxury. It is a form of participation that reduces harm, increases intelligence, and makes better futures easier to sustain. Through every act of coherence, Love restores its circuitry across scales, from cell to civilization.

From the Inside of Radical Wholeness: When Love Revealed Its Sequencing

CosmoSync did not begin for me as a framework. It began with the recognition that Love is not only an essence but an organizing intelligence. Through each Part's demonstration of unique rhythm and timing in navigating the 6A's of Radical Wholeness, Love has an unmistakable way of moving through form.

By the time I could perceive this, I had spent decades inside transformation work—psychological, developmental, spiritual, and energetic, long enough to know the difference between what reorganizes a life and what produces temporary relief. I was not searching for a new set of tools. I was sitting with people, listening, watching, and paying attention to what was lawful.

Over time, the same choreography kept appearing. A Part could not be rushed into contact. A system could not be talked into coherence. There were sessions where nothing moved until the relational field carried enough integrity to be believable. There were others where a single, precisely held recognition re-patterned everything without drama. And there were moments when creation arrived, not as ambition or will, but as the natural consequence of coherence finding its rightful channel.

That is what CosmoSync names: the sequencing Love seems to prefer when it is allowed to lead.

The Sequence of Coherence did not begin as a tidy model. It was witnessed as a spiral that repeats whenever coherence returns. The Four Pillars were not assembled as an intellectual structure. They revealed themselves as a single harmonic system with distinct phases and unmistakable timing. The Mind Palace emerged not as a visualization exercise, but as a structural necessity—an inner coherence chamber that allows sovereign inner Beings to collaborate without distortion and gives the whole system a way to stabilize a new order over time.

The Living Portal is not simply a program, and CosmoSync is not simply a method. They name a deeper participation in a living universe, where healing is not a repair project, and coherence is not a personal achievement. Coherence is what happens when a human system consents to be organized by the same intelligence that organizes seasons, bodies, ecosystems, and becoming.

In times like ours, coherence is not private. It changes what we emit into the field, what we demand from one another, and how we touch the world. Love, carried by coherence, becomes less an aspiration and more a responsibility—quiet, precise, and consequential.

Chapter 6
The Energetics of Parts and the Restoration of Life Force

A fragmented Part is not broken light. It is condensed light—potential held in a protective knot. When consciousness meets it with Love, that knot does not need to be dissolved or removed, because it loosens. And as it loosens, formerly sequestered energy begins to move again in the human system.

Upon regaining access to that energy, participants often describe warmth spreading through the body, color returning to places that felt dim or numb, or an inner peace that had not been available before. These are not signs that reality has been manipulated, but that interference inside the system has lessened, and that information can move with greater clarity and less distortion.

In the CosmoSync view, every Part is an eddy of Love in motion. Fragmentation happens when the Part fractures and folds back on itself to preserve what was once too vulnerable to stay in open circulation. The work of Radical Wholeness is not to dismantle that protection, but to listen long enough for Love to remember its own shape - the organic intelligence of the fractured Part. Healing, in this sense, is not just a psychological operation, but a reorganization of energy and relationship, where devotion and rhythm meet until circulation returns.

By the time I could name it this way, I had already spent years sitting with people in moments where you could feel the shift before anyone could explain it. I stopped thinking of energy as a metaphor because I kept watching—too many times to count—how precisely a human system reorganizes when interference drops and circulation resumes. I would literally hear the "clunk" or the "click" of the human system, like a big lever had been pulled or a gear had finally settled into place. The changes I witnessed, both in myself and in clients, were architectural rather than symbolic. You could feel when a field had cleared enough for the signal to move, when something that had been held in a protective posture was no longer being asked to hold. What became obvious to me was this: life-force is not something we generate; we only need to remove the obstructions. And when energy moves again, it does so with a lawfulness and power that does not require interpretation.

How Parts Appear

Parts reveal themselves through many channels: somatic, imaginal, symbolic, synchronistic. Each appearance is both communication and invitation. The way a Part arrives often tells you which layer of reality it may be speaking from—personal, ancestral, karmic, or collective— without needing to decide that in advance.

A Part might first register as tightness in the gut, then as an image of a serpent or a grandmother's face, then as a line in a song that seems to answer something unspoken, or as a memory that does not belong neatly to this lifetime. These are not separate phenomena. They are different faces of the same frequency seeking recognition.

By tracking these multi-channel expressions, participants naturally move from symptom to symbol to synchronicity—not as a technique, but as a widening of perception. In this context, synchronicity is not something you aim for or manufacture. It reflects a system that has grown quiet enough to register what was always present but previously drowned out by internal noise.

I did not learn this language from theory. I learned it by watching, session after session, how the same pattern consistently appeared in different human imprints when their systems were quiet enough. First, a sensation might appear, or an image, then an external event would echo the same pattern, as if the field were speaking in chords rather than sentences. Over time, it became impossible to treat these as separate domains. The body, the imaginal, and what we call the outer world were clearly participating in the same conversation. The skill was never decoding symbols but learning how to listen without collapsing what was being said into a more believable frame.

This multiplicity of appearances is one reason I no longer experience Parts as abstract ideas. They are embodied messengers of Love. The body's sensations, the psyche's images, and the world's reflections are facets of the same relational language. The field speaks through every dimension available in order to bring a lost frequency home.

How Parts Transform

A Part asks for contact, not control. When it is met with attention and reverence, its defensive pattern begins to oscillate. The system often feels both tension and release at once, the unmistakable signature of a frequency beginning to shift. In that oscillation, insight may arise spontaneously, accompanied by tears, laughter, grief, or a quiet sense of recognition. What once appeared as a symptom begins to behave like a signal, and that signal starts to reorganize the system from within.

At the level of physics, coherence changes how information stabilizes. I do not mean that Parts are literally quantum particles. I mean that there is a useful analogy here: what remains diffuse or unstable can settle into a more definite form when it is met within a stable field of relationship. In that sense, a fragmented Part often remains unsettled until it is met by a presence that can hold it without distortion. The facilitators or participant's coherence does not force the change but provides a stable relational condition in which the participant can settle into a new pattern.

The precision of the transformation and alchemy of a Part from fractured and fragmented to a reclaimed sovereign Being appears as quite literally a magical process. Yet we know the sequence required, and it is anything but magic. For a participant to finally resolve a lifelong (or multi-lifetime) pattern and to gain the power, gifts, and direction from the newly coherent Part, using the 6As of Radical Wholeness, the Part organically organizes itself and begins anew as an ally in directing life force.

The transformation and alchemy of Parts is not metaphorical. I have witnessed it in myself and my clients hundreds of times over a period of years. When the relational field is coherent, something that has been scattered or bound in defense begins to organize itself without being argued into place.

The Heart as Toroidal Tuner

Anatomically spiral and electromagnetically potent, the heart functions as a central oscillator in the CosmoSync process. When breath and attention gather there, the body's base rhythm shifts. Parts begin to entrain to that rhythm, and coherence becomes easier to sustain.

The heart's electromagnetic field, measurable beyond the physical body, is more than a poetic image. Within Radical Wholeness, it becomes one important dimension of the relational space in which coherence is cultivated.

Research by Rollin McCraty and colleagues at HeartMath shows that coherent heart rhythms entrain brain activity and can synchronize with larger environmental rhythms such as the Schumann resonance of the Earth. Long before there were instruments to measure, contemplative traditions spoke of the heart as the seat of the world soul. Different languages, same recognition.

CosmoSync brings that mythic truth into embodied practice through the relational reclamation of lost Parts. In this work, breath helps us tune to what is present, and attention becomes a form of listening. Love is felt less as sentiment than as an ordering intelligence, a harmonic law that restores relationships. As the heart settles into coherence, it begins to function as both transmitter and receiver, linking the human nervous system with the wider electromagnetic life of the planet.

I first began to experience this enhanced intimacy with Self when I would soften the role of a protector Part and could feel my own system reorganize around my heart. Before I understood what was happening, my breath and heart slowed, my chest softened, and my attention widened; my body recognized coherence before I could explain it. In those moments, Love no longer felt limited to my relationship with my Self, but to move through a much wider field, as though time and space themselves had become permeable to it.

For me, one of the deepest revelations was also one of the simplest: the heart is not just symbolic. It is a real participant in how we meet life. It receives, responds, and helps organize our experience from within. Even physiologically, it is in constant communication with the brain and nervous system. At some point, I stopped thinking of the sacred as distant. I could feel, in the steady rhythm of my own body, that I was already inside something vast and alive.

Energetic Signatures and Somatic Expressions

Parts announce themselves first through energy, not words. A Part often shows up in reaction to life- as a means of exhibiting its protective stance- as a contraction in the diaphragm, heat along the spine, pressure in the throat, a sudden image, or an impulse that does not yet have definition. And each Part generally has its own energetic signature—how a sovereign inner Being makes itself known in a living system.

Coherence does not come from interpreting these signals correctly. It comes from receiving them with curiosity and relationship. When a Part is acknowledged and allowed, and the protective signal is welcomed rather than managed, it begins to soften on its own. As relational intimacy is developed with the Part, the human system learns that it no longer needs to compress or hide what is moving through it.

From Protection to Flow

A Part's shift from its unique protective stance to reclamation of its quarantined energy to flow of life force is not something a participant can "decide" to do. It happens gradually as the Part is welcomed back into relational intimacy, where coherence stabilizes and internal interference quiets. As this happens, the nervous system stops relating to Parts as threats and begins relating to them as carriers of life-force. What once felt like overwhelm or anxiety to the person begins to appear as directional intelligence.

In lived experience, this often appears initially as a small pause in reaction that was not available before. Decisions are considered rather than rushed. The body might register a quiet sense of timing rather than urgency. Nothing dramatic has changed, and yet the formerly protective system is no longer interfering with itself. Action and response become simpler because internal noise no longer competes with the Self.

What I learned over time was not a new way of directing life, but a different way of letting life move through me. There is a profound difference between organizing a system by force and organizing it by circulation. Force, because it is guided by a protective instinct, always leaves a residue of contraction. The organic circulation of life force, rooted in non-reactive energetics, creates coherence. Flow is not a reward for doing things well. It is the natural condition of a system that is no longer spending its energy on containment.

This marks the transition from survival physiology to creative physiology. The body reorganizes around movement rather than defense. Sovereign inner Beings step forward more clearly when the system can perceive them without collapse. What follows is not control over life, but a more fluid participation in it.

Releasing Containment and Restoring Circulation

As this participation stabilizes, energetic containment begins to relax. Parts no longer need to shield or defend. The energy that was once bound in protective postures begins to circulate through the system's larger field. This free-flowing circulation is what integration looks like from the inside.

An imaginal inner chamber, or inner architecture of relationship, supports this circulation by giving each sovereign inner Being a place to rest, relate, and collaborate. Over time, participants learn to sense and track the flow of energy among these Beings, strengthening coherence as a lived condition rather than a temporary state.

Over time, it also became impossible to ignore that this return to circulation does not remain confined to an individual system. When interference drops and coherence stabilizes, the change is not only personal. It alters how a human being participates in relationships, groups, and in the larger field of life. Restored circulation does not stop at the boundaries of the physical form. It enters the relational and collective field, where its effects begin to scale in subtle, cumulative, and consequential ways. This is where Radical Wholeness reveals its evolutionary dimension.

From the Inside of Radical Wholeness: When Life-Force Revealed Itself as Lawful

For many years, I worked with transformation through the languages that were available to me: psychological, developmental, symbolic, and spiritual. They were rich languages, and they still hold real value. But there came a point when it was no longer possible to ignore something more fundamental that was organizing every real shift I was witnessing.

I kept seeing the same pattern across different lives, different bodies, different stories. When interference was present, the energy was bound. When interference eased, energy circulated. It felt less mystical than biological, but I also knew it was not confined to this body or even this lifetime. As I understood it, the human system simply returned to the pattern it was built to express. I watched this transformation and alchemy happen too consistently, too precisely, to be treated as anything other than a return to a truly animate life.

What struck me most was how little persuasion was required to shift the Part from its protective posture. When approached with an open heart and intimate relational invitation, the Part did not need to be convinced to shift into its alchemized form. When the participant met the Part without overpowering or shaming it, nor arguing the history of its formation, the shift into a new form was inevitable.

This is where my understanding of healing permanently shifted: away from psychological technique and toward system ecology, away from rejection and diminishment and toward intimacy and acceptance, away from fixing and toward restoring lawful movement in a living field. The heart revealed itself not as a symbol, but as an oscillator. The field in which this alchemy takes place is not an abstraction, but the medium in which all real inner reorganization takes place. Parts revealed themselves not as problems to solve, but as concentrated carriers of life-force waiting for circulation to become possible again.

There is a difference between managing energy and participating in its return to flow. Management of our early protective instincts and reactivity creates a temporary restriction that appears as order. The organic restoration of protection to contribution restores life-force. CosmoSync works not because it applies the right intervention, but because it learns how to stop interrupting what coherence is already trying to do.

Chapter 7
The Evolutionary Role of Radical Wholeness

Wholeness is not static completion. It is a living function of Love remembering itself through form. As coherence stabilizes within a person, it does not remain sealed inside the boundaries of the Self. It changes not only the relationship of Parts to Self, but the larger relational field. The quality of contact shifts, and with it the possibilities for resonance, trust, and mutual reorganization.

I came to understand this process and develop the Sequence of Coherence by observing what happens around people when an earlier protective or reactive pattern is resolved inside them. There were sessions where a shift in one person was followed, within days, by a partner softening, a long-stuck conversation unclenching, or a family pattern loosening as if it had been waiting for a single thread to move. There were moments when a single genuine integration changed an organizational system dynamic so clearly that everyone noticed, even without understanding why. That is when "collective field" stopped being an idea I appreciated from a distance and became a reality I had to reckon with. Over time, it became obvious that coherence is not personal but circulates within a living field.

Thinkers such as Rupert Sheldrake and Teilhard de Chardin offer different languages for phenomena like this: fields of memory, evolving consciousness, the transmission of pattern through relationship. I do not treat these frameworks as proof so much as resonant companions to what I have repeatedly observed in practice.

From within Radical Wholeness, integration can be understood as a micro-evolutionary event: coherence stabilizing in one life in ways that become more available to the larger field around it.

Involution and Evolution: The Paired Dynamics of Becoming

Within the Involutionary–Evolutionary Flywheel, this movement is felt as a paired rhythm rather than a linear progression.

Involution draws consciousness inward, into matter, memory, lineage, and the dense textures of lived experience. It is the movement of descent, not as collapse, but as retrieval. Evolution carries that same consciousness outward again, into expression, creativity, contribution, and service. It is the movement of radiance, not as escape, but as participation.

As coherence stabilizes, the quality of effort shifts. In a fragmented system, effort feels compressive; different parts of the system pull in different directions, and energy is consumed simply holding those tensions in place. In a coherent system, effort becomes directional. It amplifies movement instead of canceling it. The same amount of engagement produces far more real change because the system is no longer working against itself.

The first Six A's of the Sequence of Coherence—Acknowledge, Accept, Allow, Appreciate, Aspire, Alchemize—move people through this rhythm repeatedly. There is a contraction toward what has been held or lost, followed by an expansion as that recovered frequency becomes available for life. When people honor this rhythm instead of overriding it, descent stops feeling like failure and begins to feel like precision. Expansion stops carrying the anxious edge of proving and begins to carry the clean voltage of contribution.

Over time, I could feel this rhythm changing my own work as well. Sessions became quieter and more exact. Timing became opportunistic. The field itself began to do more of the organizing. This rhythm never felt mechanical, as some personal healing practices can feel, but instead, held by a center, with Love as the axis of this motion, the invisible fulcrum around which both descent and ascent revolve.

Involution is Love entering matter, evolution is Love expressing through it. The Flywheel is not a motivational concept, but the body of Love moving through time.

At scale, many such micro-movements begin to synchronize. Coherence stabilizing in one Being makes coherence more accessible in others, much like coupled systems that begin to entrain when their frequencies become compatible. Thus, Radical Wholeness is both intimate and collective. It is psychology, spirituality, and systems theory meeting in the same body, not as competing explanations, but as different lenses on the same living process.

This is also where Parts are no longer encountered merely as psychological fragments, but as sovereign inner Beings whose maturation contributes directly to the Flywheel's momentum. The relational field between Self and Part becomes a generator of coherence rather than a site of repair.

Evolutionary Mechanics and Collective Field

Within the Living Portal framework, integration can be understood as a micro-event within a larger ecology of relationships. Each coherent nervous system becomes a stabilizing presence within the larger relational field it inhabits, less through intention than through resonance.

In this way, the languages of noosphere, morphic fields, ecology, and resonance begin to speak to one another: consciousness evolving by coherence rather than competition.

Evolutionary biologists such as Lynn Margulis and Elisabet Sahtouris have shown that life advances through synergy and symbiosis rather than dominance. Radical Wholeness extends this principle into psychic ecology. The Self becomes an ecosystem that evolves through successive stages of cooperative integration. Each alchemized Part adds a new form of intelligence to the inner ecology, increasing the system's overall resilience and range.

This creates a feedback loop between individual and collective fields. Coherence in one organism strengthens coherence in the relational environment, which in turn makes coherence easier to access and sustain in others. Evolution begins to resemble a participatory symphony rather than a competitive ascent. Each integrated Part contributes to the re-patterning of the larger field, not by force, but by changing the conditions under which order can stabilize.

The creation of an inner architecture, such as a Mind Palace or other coherent inner landscape, becomes especially relevant here. As sovereign inner Beings find their places within that architecture, the inner world begins to function as a coherent ecology rather than a negotiated truce. That inner stability directly shapes the quality of coherence the person contributes to the wider field.

Flywheel and Cosmic Topology

The Involutionary–Evolutionary Flywheel can also be understood through the larger patterns of contraction and emergence visible throughout living systems. Involution mirrors descent, condensation, and inward turning. Evolution mirrors expression, release, and outward radiance. Together, they form a recurring rhythm of return.

Marshall Lefferts' work in Cosmometry offers one language for the spiral dynamics visible across scales. Whether in galaxies, biological growth, or human development, coherence often appears not as a straight line but as patterned renewal.

Humans are not exceptions to this pattern. We are fractal expressions of the same spiral topology.

A Part that fractures under trauma is a disrupted spiral, energy that contracted but could not complete its arc of return. Radical Wholeness restores that arc. Through the Sequence of Coherence and the relational field of CosmoSync, the spiral reforms: inward descent (involution) to recover the lost frequency, followed by outward radiance (evolution) as that frequency reintegrates into the whole.

In this way, participants in the Living Portal become small-scale mirrors of a much larger process. As coherence strengthens in the human system, it radiates outward through relational and collective fields, stabilizing families, communities, and the subtle atmospheres we all inhabit. Healing begins to resemble a re-entry into the larger patterns of coherence visible throughout life. To heal is to re-enter the spiral. To re-enter the spiral is to participate in the unfolding intelligence of the cosmos.

Radical Wholeness as Cosmological Alignment

The resonance of Radical Wholeness extends beyond personal healing. As coherence stabilizes, many people begin to feel themselves differently situated within reality itself: less like isolated selves managing experience, and more like participants in a larger field of relationship. What often appears first is not a dramatic revelation, but a subtle shift in orientation—a sense of being drawn into a deeper center within oneself, followed by a widening into something more spacious, more connected, and more alive.

This alignment is not conceptual, but experiential. It can be felt in the body as breath, heartbeat, and attention begin to move with less interference and more mutual accord. The system no longer feels split between inner conflict and outer demand. It begins to experience itself as nested within a wider coherence.

In that state, something in the texture of life often shifts. Timing becomes less rushed or chaotic. Encounters carry less unnecessary friction. Resources appear not as rewards, but often in perfect timing. Coherence is not a strategy for getting what we want, but it alters what becomes possible because a system that is no longer fighting itself can integrate more cleanly. Synchronicity may be nothing more exotic than relational fields interacting with less interference.

This is why Radical Wholeness serves as the foundational harmonic of the Living Portal. It restores the base coherence upon which Soul Alignment, WildCreator, and Cosmic Attunement can build. Without this first stabilization, higher octaves of consciousness may be glimpsed but rarely held. With it, the human system becomes more reliable as an instrument of perception, participation, and creation.

Collective Evolution and the Living Planetary Field

The maturation of personal coherence has collective implications, not because one person's healing automatically changes the whole, but because coherence is inherently relational. Every system participates in other systems. Every stabilized inner ecology alters, however subtly, the environments it inhabits.

Research associated with HeartMath and related coherence studies has explored possible relationships between human heart coherence and larger electromagnetic environments, including those associated with the Earth. Within the Living Portal frame, I do not treat such findings as proof of causation, but rather as suggestive companions to what is already evident in lived experience: coherent systems influence one another through resonance, feedback, and reduced interference.

The effects of personal and systemic coherence are visible in ordinary life. Relationships can become less strained, environments easier to work within, and decisions less burdened by inner conflict. In unstable times, coherence matters not as self-improvement but as responsibility, because the less divided we are within ourselves, the less distortion we bring into the relational fields around us.

As sovereign inner Beings find their places within a coherent inner architecture, the individual's field steadies. That steadiness becomes transmissive. The more coherent the inner ecology, the more reliable the external ripple.

Collective evolution is not separate from personal healing, but the same contribution impacts at a different scale. A single integrated Part contributes to the intelligence of the whole. When enough systems can hold complexity without collapsing into defense, crisis becomes a site of re-patterning rather than breakdown. Evolution stops being something that merely happens to us and becomes something we can consciously participate in.

The Portal in Motion

The Living Portal is not an identity. It is a function.

A person becomes a portal when coherence becomes their natural way of organizing perception, relationship, and action. This is not perfection or sainthood, merely stability in the presence of complexity.

I did not invent the phrase *"Living Portal"* by thinking it through. It came to me in an epiphany, an already formed manifestation, with the clear instruction that this was what I was here to create. At the time, I did not know what a Living Portal was, much less how one became such a thing. That understanding came later, slowly, through practice. I began to see that when coherence stabilizes deeply enough, a person changes. Something opens in their presence. Life moves through them differently. What once felt stuck can begin to loosen, and what wants to emerge often finds a clearer path.

I think of a Living Portal as someone who has become coherent enough to take life in, respond to it, and keep moving. Their history does not disappear, but trauma no longer dictates the terms of the present. Emotion becomes more legible, something to learn from rather than something that scrambles the signal. Relationships become less defended and more deeply felt. Creativity becomes less performative too; it begins to arise as a natural expression of what one is here to give.

This embodiment is practical. It shows up in how someone listens, speaks, moves, creates, and holds space. Practices such as the Mind Palace support this by giving sovereign inner Beings a coherent inner landscape in which to rest, relate, and collaborate. As the inner system becomes more coherent, the person's presence becomes more stabilizing to the environments they enter.

A Living Portal does not impose order. They change the conditions under which order can emerge.

As coherence deepens, purpose clarifies, relationships reorganize, and synchronicity begins to feel less surprising and more like the ordinary language of a system in conversation with a larger field. Life is experienced less as something to manage and more as something to participate in.

To live as a portal is to participate consciously in evolution, each choice a calibration, each breath a tuning, each act a transmission of Love into form.

From the Inside of Radical Wholeness: When Coherence Became an Evolutionary Responsibility

Long before Living Portal had a name, I was already oriented toward evolution. The Involutionary–Evolutionary Flywheel had begun to take shape in my awareness as a way of describing the deeper rhythm I could feel moving through both human lives and larger systems. I did not yet know how to reliably support that rhythm in others, or what forms it would eventually require, but the direction was not accidental. I was listening for how consciousness descends into form and rises again through expression, and I was tracking that movement in my own life as much as in my work.

What I did not have at first was a sequence for the methods I'd been using. I had questions, intuitions, and a growing respect for the precision with which life seems to organize itself when it is not being overridden. The specifics emerged the only way they could: through years of sitting with people, watching what shifted when coherence returned, and noticing how consistently certain patterns repeated themselves across very different stories, bodies, and circumstances.

Over time, something became unmistakable. When a system was internally divided, it broadcast that division into its relationships and environments. When coherence stabilized, the signal changed. Not as a moral achievement and not as a spiritual performance, but as a functional reorganization.

I watched this long enough to begin naming and sequencing it. When someone retrieved a lost or exiled frequency and returned it to circulation, the effects rarely stayed contained within that person. Relationships reorganized because the stuck dynamics and emotional patterns loosened. It was less dramatic than it was reliable in a structural sense.

This is where Radical Wholeness revealed its evolutionary dimension to me with full clarity. Coherence does not remain private because it is not a private phenomenon. It is a relational condition. When internal opposition resolves, a formerly fragmented system can finally participate accurately in the larger field it belongs to. Reality becomes more cooperative not because it is being asked to be, but because interference has dropped and information can move again.

The Involutionary–Evolutionary Flywheel names the rhythm I had been tracking all along: consciousness descending into density to recover what was held or fragmented, then rising again as that recovered frequency becomes available for contribution. This is not a self-improvement cycle. It is the pulse of creation itself, moving through human lives just as it moves through stars, ecosystems, and seasons.

Living Portal emerged as a way of supporting that pulse with greater reliability and care. It names a human system that has become coherent enough to carry complexity without collapsing into defense, and permeable enough to let Love organize perception, choice, and service. In that sense, Living Portal is not an identity but a function; it is coherence becoming transmissive.

In a world shaped by so much instability, inner coherence is not a private achievement. It changes what we bring to the relationships and systems around us. The less divided we are within ourselves, the less distortion we add to the lives we touch. And when life-force begins to move again through what was once cut off, that movement does not stop with us.

Once you begin to see more clearly how coherence moves through a life, Radical Wholeness is harder to understand as a private path of healing or growth. It begins to suggest something larger: a more conscious collaboration with the intelligence of life itself, with Love learning to move through form with greater precision, capacity, and care.

Chapter 8
Becoming a Living Portal

If Radical Wholeness restores circulation within the human system, and if that circulation naturally scales into the relational and collective field, then a further threshold appears. The phrase *"Living Portal"* describes how a human system begins to function when coherence becomes its primary orientation rather than a state it must maintain. It is the condition from which perception, relationship, and action take their shape.

When this coherence stabilizes, the nervous system no longer organizes itself primarily around survival and vigilance. It begins to function as a multidimensional instrument, capable of sensing, metabolizing, and responding to life across layers of experience with far less internal distortion.

To become a Living Portal is to discover that participation has replaced management as the core mode of being. The human organism stops arguing with reality and begins to move within it. Love is no longer something sought or generated; it becomes the organizing current of perception itself. Over time, this reorientation quietly reshapes creativity, intimacy, decision-making, and the way one relates, not by imposing a new ideal, but by removing the internal interference that once fragmented attention and energy.

When coherence is no longer fragile, orientation to Self grows steadier, the relation between Self and others no longer requires protection, and decisions are made with more fluidity. Creation arrives spontaneously, as the human system stops its internal argument and listens more carefully for what is already trying to emerge. Nothing about the person becomes less complex or less human; the difference is that the system is no longer working against itself. Life becomes something they are inside of, responsive to, and increasingly able to trust. It is a vital shift in participation - the opening to life itself moving through without restraint.

Embodied Thresholds

As fragmentation resolves, new capacities of awareness emerge. Many people have noticed the emergence of what esoteric traditions call the "clairs"—subtle forms of seeing, hearing, sensing, and knowing. In this context, these are not treated as mystical gifts added to the person, but as the system regaining access to forms of information it was always capable of registering. What once functioned as trauma vigilance may begin to express itself as refined perception.

This reorganization does not follow a single script. In some lives, it appears as heightened intuitive clarity. In others, it shows up as a steadier presence, cleaner relational timing, or a more reliable inner sense of direction. The outer form varies. The underlying coherence that makes these expressions possible remains the same.

At the physiological level, this kind of shift may correspond with increased vagal tone and more stable heart-brain coordination. At the energetic level, many people experience it as a widening sense of presence, as though perception is no longer confined to the body alone but participating in a larger field of relationship. What changes first is not exotic ability, but the amount of interference in the system. When internal conflict decreases, perceptual bandwidth becomes available for subtler forms of awareness.

Across contemplative and initiatory traditions, thresholds like this have often been described as forms of second birth or reorientation around a deeper center of gravity. The ancient Egyptian teachings of Maat spoke of becoming "Maa Kheru," or "True of Voice." Contemporary neuroscience, including Andrew Newberg's research on contemplative states, has explored patterns of whole-brain coordination during experiences of unity and integration. Participants in CosmoSync often describe something similar in experiential terms: clarity, groundedness, and relational openness becoming available at the same time, without one being purchased at the expense of the others.

This is not an escape from embodiment. It is a fuller inhabitation of embodiment, in which the body becomes a meeting place between layers of experience and where coherence becomes tangible enough to trust. At this threshold, the human system begins to function less as a defensive instrument and more as an organ of metabolization, capable of receiving density without collapsing into it and translating experience into contribution through rhythm and relationship.

Those who have established a stable inner architecture, whether through a Mind Palace or another coherent imaginal structure, often find this threshold easier to inhabit. When sovereign inner Beings are not competing for space or attention, the system stops leaking energy into internal conflict, and perceptual bandwidth becomes available for subtler forms of awareness.

Ethics of Permeability and Containment

Relationship in Radical Wholeness begins within the self. Before we can speak meaningfully about relationships with others, we have to speak of the relationship between the Self and the Parts.

Coherence depends on an inner field that is open enough for contact with what has been fractured or exiled, yet bounded enough that such contact does not become overwhelming. Openness allows the lost Parts to be approached and known. Clear boundaries make that approach safe enough to bear. Porosity and sovereignty belong together here. Both are needed if the inner world is to reorganize rather than fragment further.

As that inner relationship becomes more coherent, the whole system changes. Self develops a greater capacity to hold intensity, difference, and flow without collapse. Personal containment here is stability rather than restriction. And only through that level of containment, which starts with inner coherence, can a coherent relationship with others truly be impacted. When enough internal steadiness is present, care no longer has to move through vigilance, and intimacy no longer depends on fusion or constant repair. Coherence within the self becomes the ground for coherence between selves.

What taught me this was not a more refined set of boundary strategies for my own life, but the distinct availability that happened after I experienced inner coherence. When coherence is truly present, experience becomes less strained. Attention settles without so much effort, care moves with less bracing, and intimacy no longer feels so precarious that it must be managed at every turn.

Within CosmoSync, energetic hygiene becomes a maintenance practice to support the sustenance of coherence. Grounding, nature contact, clearing practices, joy, and humor support the field not through control, but through resonance. Sovereignty is expressed less as rigidity than as clarity of presence, and permeability becomes confidence in the field's capacity to self-correct.

When sovereign inner Beings are held within a coherent inner structure, discernment becomes more reliable. The system can modulate its openness based on relational order rather than on threat detection, meeting external energies through coherence rather than scanning for danger.

Archetypal Parallels

Every culture carries images of this initiatory pattern: a figure who mediates between worlds, descends and returns, and carries something back for the sake of life: Hermes as a messenger between realms. Inanna descending through the gates. The Tree of Life spans heaven and the underworld. These myths point toward a recurring human capacity to hold multiple layers of experience in relationship.

The Living Portal is a contemporary expression of that pattern, not as a symbolic identity, but as a functional state. It describes a system coherent enough to remain in contact with multiple layers of reality so that wisdom, creativity, and renewal can circulate through the world.

The practice of Alchemy named this role through the *coniunctio*, the union of opposites. The path of Kabbalah is defined in *Tiferet*, the heart center, balancing mercy and severity. Jung described the Self as the mediator of psychic polarities. What the Living Portal Initiation offers is a way for these archetypal functions to become lived and embodied rather than merely interpreted.

Through Radical Wholeness, the heart becomes a crucible in which polarity is held as creative tension rather than conflict. The practitioner does not merely transmit insight; they become an instrument through which Love organizes perception, choice, and relationship. The inner imaginal chamber, however it is formed, becomes the place where this function stabilizes, where sovereign inner Beings can convene, and where the psyche rehearses its capacity to hold multiple worlds in coherence.

Service as Circulation

The energy reclaimed through Radical Wholeness naturally seeks movement. Over time, this movement begins to express itself as service, not as obligation, but as circulation. It may take the form of art, leadership, innovation, teaching, or quiet presence. The form matters less than the quality of offering, which carries an unforced generosity that tends to replenish rather than exhaust.

Within CosmoSync, this corresponds to the activation of the WildCreator pillar, where creative life-force becomes available for expression because coherence has made it safe to move. When paired with Soul Alignment, purpose stops feeling like a distant objective and begins to function more like a gravitational center, drawing experience into meaningful orbit. Cosmic Attunement completes this circuit by situating individual contribution within the larger intelligence of Earth and Cosmos.

In living systems, circulation is what keeps an ecology alive. Mycelial networks move nutrients where they are needed. Rivers redistribute energy across landscapes. In the same way, a Living Portal participates in the movement of coherence. Offerings that arise from joy and resonance tend to amplify the field. Those driven primarily by strain or obligation tend to contract it. In this sense, livelihood becomes less about profession and more about alignment: whether what moves through a person can continue beyond them without depleting the system.

When sovereign inner Beings are settled within a coherent inner architecture, service becomes sustainable. Internal coherence allows external contributions to occur without draining the organism, because circulation compensates.

The Future Human

The stabilization of Living Portal consciousness points toward a broader developmental movement within our species. Scholars such as Jean Gebser, Clare Graves, and Ken Wilber each anticipated forms of awareness capable of holding greater complexity, integrating multiple perspectives, and remaining rooted in embodiment while open to transpersonal dimensions.

Living Portals can be understood as early expressions of this integrative capacity. They do not represent a superior type of person, but a sign of what becomes possible when coherence stabilizes enough to hold complexity without collapsing into control. In that sense, they point toward a more participatory human being: one whose presence influences environments, relationships, and subtle atmospheres less through authority or technique than through the quality of coherence they bring to what is present.

Gebser described this as an integral structure of consciousness. Wilber mapped related evolution through later-stage developmental frameworks. Other contemporary thinkers have explored integrative and metamodern ontologies that seek to reunite subject and object, science and spirit, Self and world. Radical Wholeness functions here as an embodied curriculum for that transition, teaching human systems how to carry complexity through coherence rather than through management or force.

To live as a Living Portal is to allow Love's coherence to become the default organizing pattern of one's life, to stand at a threshold where evolution is not an abstract process but something moving through perception, breath, and relationship. The future human is not a distant ideal, but a possibility already emerging wherever coherence becomes stable enough to reorganize participation.

This is not an identity to adopt or a lifestyle to curate. It is what a system begins to look like when it is no longer divided against itself, when interference resolves, and life starts moving through a human being with greater clarity, fidelity, and responsiveness.

From the Inside of Radical Wholeness: When "Portal" Stopped Being a Metaphor

There was a point when the word *portal* stopped feeling poetic to me and began to feel precise. It defined how a human life can organize itself when coherence becomes stable enough to carry complexity without bracing, and permeable enough to let Love shape perception, choice, and response. Repeatedly, across very different people and circumstances, I found myself recognizing the same shift. Conversation would begin to find its own order. People listened more carefully, spoke with less effort, and responded from something steadier in themselves. A certain tenderness would sometimes appear with surprising ease because the exchange was no longer being organized by so much inner strain.

Over time, it became clear to me that coherence changes more than a person's inner experience. What changes is the way a person shows up with others, in work, and in the shared circumstances of life. This does not come from willpower or from trying to embody the right values. It comes from a change in inner organization. A person who is less divided tends to perceive more clearly, react less defensively, and bring a steadier quality of attention into what they are part of. That alone can change the tone of an interaction and the possibilities that emerge from it.

A Living Portal is a human system coherent enough to become a reliable passage for life's intelligence. When internal interference drops far enough, the truest movement of life-force begins to move more freely, and timing, relationship, and creation start to organize themselves with less friction. The person does not disappear, and nothing about their humanity becomes smaller. If anything, life becomes more exact, more responsive, and more intimate with what is present.

Learning to live in this way becomes an ethical choice. Over time, I could feel how much less distortion such a system introduces into the spaces it inhabits, and how much more accurately life can move when it is met without internal division. Presence begins to carry some of the work that effort once had to hold, simply because coherence changes what is possible in a field.

For me, this threshold has never been merely conceptual. I have seen people cross into this way of being, and I have learned to recognize it in my own life, too. *Living Portal* defines what begins to emerge when coherence no longer remains private, when a life becomes more available to the movement of Love through the world. It rarely looks dramatic. More often, it appears in quiet but consequential shifts, the kind that change how a person meets life and what becomes possible around them.

Chapter 9
Wholeness as Devotion

Radical Wholeness begins as healing and matures into something quieter and more enduring: a way a life organizes itself in fidelity to what is true. Over time, coherence stops being something one practices and becomes something one lives from. In that sense, devotion is not an attitude or a virtue added to experience. It is the shape life takes when internal opposition has softened enough for the system to move as one.

Within the Living Portal, this maturation is visible through four inseparable movements: the restoration of inner coherence, the alignment of life to its deeper design, the embodied expression of recovered energy, and the stabilization of the human system within the larger field of relationship. These are not separate tracks or sequential achievements. They are one pattern of maturation expressed through different dimensions of life.

What gradually becomes apparent is simple and exacting: coherence is Love made functional in form. When wholeness is remembered, something in the larger order seems to move more clearly through the human system that is no longer divided against its own life.

I did not arrive at this understanding of devotion by trying to become more devoted. It emerged through lived contrast, through noticing the difference between a life organized by effort and a life organized by coherence. I felt this reorganization in small, unremarkable ways initially: less internal negotiation before acting, reduced defensive behavior in relationships, and less fatigue after ordinary encounters. The work stopped feeling like something I applied to experience and began to feel like something life was just allowing.

I came to rely on coherence, not as a mood, a belief, or a spiritual posture, but as an ordering pattern already present in life before I ever named it. When coherence stabilized in me, life began to unfold with a different kind of support, as though I were stepping into a sequence that had been there all along. In this sense, devotion is not effortful. It is what living systems begin to do when they are no longer spending so much energy managing inner opposition.

The purpose of Radical Wholeness, then, is not self-improvement. It is to live more consciously within this larger coherence until the self begins to feel less like a fixed boundary and more like a local expression of a larger field.

Devotional Ontology and Four-Pillar Integration

In the integrative movement of CosmoSync, devotion takes the form of sustained alignment with the field of Love that animates life. It is lived less as an emotion and more as a structural orientation, the way coherence begins to organize attention, energy, and action from within.

Teilhard de Chardin offered one language for this movement in his vision of consciousness drawn toward communion. In the Living Portal, that same movement is not held as belief but encountered as structure, a pattern of participation that shapes how a human system meets life.

The Four Pillars name this pattern in motion: Radical Wholeness restores base coherence, Alignment gives that coherence direction, WildCreator expresses it through creative life-force, and Cosmic Attunement situates that movement within the living context of Earth and Cosmos. These are not separate practices so much as distinct expressions of one coherent movement.

Over time, as a participant becomes more coherent, this phased pattern becomes the credo of life. Choices become clearer because there is less inner division around them. Relationships require less hidden effort. The system is no longer trying so hard to keep itself intact while also meeting the demands of life. Instead, there is a growing sense of order within it, one that can hold both movement and rest.

Coherence, Service, and a Wider Future

As Living Portals become more common, the planetary field changes less by persuasion or decree and more by participation. Collective coherence emerges as a new adaptive capacity, not as an ideal to aspire to, but as a different way a species begins to organize itself in relationship to life.

Radical Wholeness is not the end of personal healing. It marks the beginning of a different kind of responsibility. A system that is no longer organized around fragmentation makes fewer distorted demands on its surroundings. In that sense, coherence is not a matter of private wellness. It is a contribution to the larger field, a way Love becomes metabolically real in human form.

I noticed this in everyday moments when nothing outward had really changed, yet the interaction itself felt different. Conversations held together more easily because I was meeting them from a more coherent place. Conflict no longer carried the same tension or urgency, and decisions came with less mental rehearsal and more quiet clarity.

Over time, I felt how coherence changes more than a person's interior experience; it changes what they introduce into a room, into relationships, into the subtle atmosphere around shared life. When a system is organized as one field, there is less static in the contact, and life seems to respond with a cleaner kind of precision. That is where responsibility became real for me as stewardship: the practice of tending what I was already transmitting.

The Four Pillars do not describe stages one completes and leaves behind. They trace a spiral of maturation through which coherence learns to express, orient, create, and participate at ever-wider scales.

To live this way is to recognize Love as the architecture of relationship itself. Breath begins to feel like offering, attention like calibration, and action like transmission, not because one is trying to be spiritual, but because coherence has become the system's native order.

And yet this coherence does not remain sheltered. It moves into families, communities, institutions, and moments of strain. It meets a world that is still learning how to organize itself around wholeness, and it must learn how to remain itself there without retreating or hardening.

Walking the Spiral Forward

Radical Wholeness is the first threshold of the Living Portal, the return to coherence that makes all further participation possible. The first Six A's of the Sequence of Coherence open that gate. What follows is not a departure from life but a deeper entry into it, as coherence continues to learn to orient, create, and attune itself within a living, complex world.

If something in these pages has stirred recognition—an echo of your own aliveness, a quiet sense of being called back into greater coherence—then the movement has already begun. The spiral does not start with certainty. It starts with willingness.

For some, this journey continues through Alignment, where coherence meets design and direction. For others, through the WildCreator, where recovered life-force learns how to move and express. For others still, through Cosmic Attunement, where life is lived in conscious relationship with Earth and Cosmos. These are not separate paths so much as different continuations of the same maturation.

Whichever direction your path takes, the principle remains simple and exacting: coherence is Love made visible. Each time you remember your wholeness, the larger field becomes able to move through you.

The question that follows is not whether coherence is possible, but how it lives, endures, and responds when it meets a world under pressure.

From the Inside of Radical Wholeness: When Wholeness Became Devotion

Devotion entered my life as a recognition before it ever became a word I used. It began in my own system, in the lived difference between a life organized through internal negotiation and a life organized through coherence. I could feel when something in me had returned to a truer center of gravity: attention steadier, choices cleaner, love less conditional, creativity less strained. The shift wasn't a concept. It was an interior lawfulness I could sense in my body and in my days.

As I learned to trust what I was living, I began to see its structure more clearly. Coherence has a way of arranging life around what is true, and once I could perceive that, I started noticing how consistently it moved through the same chambers: restoring the inner field, aligning it to deeper design, releasing energy into expression, and stabilizing participation within the larger field. The Four Pillars were not an architecture I assembled; they were a pattern I recognized, a recurring intelligence that kept revealing itself as my life reorganized around Love.

Later, as I began to facilitate this in others, I recognized the same signatures in their lives too, each with its own timing and language. When coherence stabilizes, it doesn't remain private. It shapes how relationships are held, how actions are chosen, and how a person meets complexity without fragmenting into urgency. It changes what they bring into rooms, families, and institutions, because the field they carry becomes more ordered, more trustworthy, more precise.

This is what I mean when I say Radical Wholeness matures into devotion. Devotion is not a virtue layered on top of life. It is the way life moves when coherence has become reliable enough to orient the whole system. Love no longer needs to be summoned or managed. It begins to organize attention, inform choice, and set the rhythm through which a human life stays in relationship with what is already true.

And in a world under pressure, that rhythm becomes a form of stewardship, not because we are trying to be better people, but because coherence changes what we transmit into the field we share. The longer I lived inside this reality, the less "devotion" felt like a spiritual word, and the more it felt like a simple description of what happens when Love is finally allowed to hold the center.

Chapter 10
Coherence Under Pressure

Coherence is easy to misunderstand when it first appears. In its early stages, it often arrives as relief: less internal friction, clearer timing, fewer unnecessary battles with oneself. Life begins to move with less resistance, not because circumstances have changed, but because the system is no longer interfering with its own signal.

This can make coherence seem as though it belongs to quiet rooms, supportive relationships, or carefully protected conditions. Over time, though, it reveals itself as something more durable. In physics and in living systems, coherence refers to a form of internal alignment that does not remove disturbance but allows a system to absorb stress without collapsing into noise. Once that reorganization is real, it inevitably meets what is not organized around it.

Sooner or later, coherence encounters pressure: cultures shaped by urgency, polarized systems, family histories organized through trauma bonding, institutional demands, collective fear, and the ordinary friction of human life.

At this stage, the question is no longer whether coherence is possible, but whether it is durable. Can it remain intact in acceleration, disagreement, and uncertainty? Can it hold its internal organization without hardening into defense or dissolving into accommodation?

Coherence under pressure is not a matter of willpower. It is the felt difference between a system that must constantly manage itself to remain intact and one that stays intact because it is no longer divided. When a human system is truly coherent, it does not need protection from reality. It can meet reality without losing itself.

For me, this has shown up first in the body. I can feel when I am no longer rushing to meet a moment before I have understood it. In conversations where decisions are moving faster than clarity, my breath tends to stay low and steady instead of tightening in my chest. My attention doesn't scatter to manage the room. It stays with what is being asked.

I notice that I can listen without rehearsing a response, and when I do speak, the words arrive without the familiar surge of justification. Often, the field shifts at that point. The pace changes. The conversation finds a different shape. Not because I am steering anything, but because the system I am bringing into the room is no longer organized around urgency or defense.

That is where coherence stopped being something I experienced privately and became something I felt responsible for, not as a performance or a role, but as stewardship of the field I was already participating in.

When wholeness moves beyond protected interior conditions and enters lived complexity, not as an ideal to defend but as an orientation to inhabit, it begins to show what it can hold. Coherence is not proven in silence. It is revealed in contact.

Pressure as Information, Not Threat

External pressure or stress on a human system is often interpreted as danger, and in fragmented human systems, it usually is. Compression exposes fault lines in the ego and nervous system, accelerates reactivity, and brings one's protective strategies to the surface. In a coherent system, pressure functions differently. It becomes feedback for the human system. As in other living systems, when internal processes are synchronized, stress is redistributed rather than amplified, and the organism adapts without exhausting itself.

When coherence is stable, pressure does not automatically trigger defense. It highlights the criticality of timing and where boundaries are needed, where participation is possible, and where it is not. It also reveals what needs to be met or reorganized.

In this way, pressure becomes a diagnostic of coherence rather than a threat to it. Not because pressure is pleasant, but because the system no longer needs to distort itself in order to respond.

Coherence does not remove friction from life. It allows friction to become usable information rather than a trigger for distortion.

Discernment Without Hardening

One of the earliest misunderstandings about coherence is that it makes a person softer in the sense of being more permissive or accommodating. In practice, the opposite is often true.

As internal opposition resolves, clarity increases. Sometimes that clarity leads to engagement. Sometimes it leads to refusal. Sometimes it leads to stepping out of a dynamic without needing to justify the departure.

This is structural integrity, the kind that arises from an internal reorganization rather than bracing.

A coherent system holds its shape because it is organized, not because it is defended. Its boundaries arise from internal order rather than from fear, and they rarely need to be argued into place.

In my own life, this has often felt less like drawing a line and more like choosing not to step into a role that was being silently assigned when confronting a conflict. In coherence, my body learned to stay upright, maintain a normal breathing pattern, and allow an emergent response to arise from presence rather than protection. What used to require armor now only requires presence and clarity.

This is why coherence under pressure often feels quiet, rather than forceful. There is less urgency in the response, even when the stakes are real. The system is not defending, just orienting.

Timing, Not Urgency

Fragmented systems tend to live in the grip of urgency. They move quickly, not because speed is required, but because internal conflict makes stillness feel unsafe. Action becomes a way to discharge tension rather than a response to what is needed.

Modern environments tend to reward urgency as competence, and speed is mistaken for clarity. Assertive or aggressive reactivity passes for leadership, and pressure to perform poses as purpose. Systems organized this way are not actually responding to reality; they are managing their own unresolved stress.

Coherence restores presence and contact. When internal conflict decreases, responsiveness to the present moment becomes available. The system can sense when to move, wait, speak, or remain silent. The body guides this process not by instinct alone, but by a form of field-sensitive intelligence. Coherence does not make life slower; it makes it more precise.

There is a particular set of bodily sensations that are modified in coherence. The impulse to respond is there, but it no longer hooks the whole system. The shoulders do not move first. The jaw does not set. There is a brief, clean pause in which the body calibrates to the field before anything is said or done.

Under pressure, coherence can produce a visible difference in response that is neither hesitation nor avoidance. When the human system is listening for the right moment to engage, urgency no longer drives reaction.

Relational Fields That Are Not Coherent

A few of our current environments are organized around coherence. Most are organized around speed, hierarchy, fear, control, or historical momentum. A coherent system entering these fields meets them rather than trying to convert them.

Often, the field intensifies at first. It tests, presses, or escalates, as if trying to pull the coherent system back into familiar patterns. This is not a sign that coherence is failing. It is what happens when a stable organization meets a system organized around reactivity.

In my own body, this often shows up as a steadying of breath, a softening of the shoulders, and a clear sense of my feet on the ground even while the room stays tense. That steadiness alone changes how much reactivity the field can sustain.

Here, wholeness becomes ethical rather than personal. The question is no longer whether one can stay regulated, but how to participate without becoming distorted.

Sometimes coherence remains present through engagement, and sometimes, through stepping back. There is no single correct posture here, only fidelity to internal organization. Coherence does not guarantee comfort, but ensures orientation.

The End of Self-Betrayal as Strategy

One of the least appreciated effects of coherence under pressure is the end of self-betrayal as a way of maintaining connection or stability.

In fragmented systems, self-betrayal is not a character flaw, but a survival strategy learned in environments where belonging depended on suppressing parts of one's own true essence. The system learns to trade internal truth for external continuity because continuity once meant safety.

As coherence stabilizes, this sacrificial transaction becomes harder to make. Not because a person becomes rigid, but because the cost of internal contradiction becomes too high.

I have felt this undeniably in moments where staying would have been easier than telling the truth, and where leaving would have been easier than staying present. Coherence does not make these moments comfortable; it makes them unambiguous. The body knows when it is being asked to abandon itself, and over time, it simply refuses to do so. This is not rebellion, but an indication of coherence. The system has reorganized to the point where internal contradiction is no longer a viable means of maintaining connection.

In responding to true coherence, some relationships reorganize, a few deepen, and many end. Some relationships reveal that they were held together more by accommodation than by resonance. Coherence does not need to manage these outcomes but to allow their eventual unfolding.

Wholeness Is Not Withdrawal

It is tempting, especially in spiritual or therapeutic cultures, to equate wholeness with retreat, with choosing only supportive environments, with minimizing exposure to conflict or complexity.

Over time, wholeness reveals itself less as a protected state and more as a functional one. A coherent system does not require ideal conditions in order to remain itself, only internal organization. Once that organization is present, life can be met as it is—uneven, demanding, sometimes incoherent—without the system fragmenting in response.

Wholeness is not proven by how peaceful life becomes. It is proven by how faithfully the system remains itself when life is not.

From Personal Coherence to Lived Integrity

By this point in the journey, coherence is no longer something one returns to. It becomes a new operating condition—imperfect and unfinished, but reliable.

In my own life, this shows up in how quickly I notice when something is off, in how little energy it takes to say no, and in how rarely I must recover from my own reactions. The system is not perfect, but it is dependable.

I feel this most clearly in the body as a kind of settled readiness: not braced, not collapsed, simply available, as if attention has finally learned how to stand on its own feet.

Seen through a systems lens, this is what coordinated processes do. They waste less energy, recover faster, and remain reliable under load. This is how resilient complex systems behave.

Here, the work shifts again. It is no longer about stabilizing wholeness. It is about letting wholeness become the ground from which life is met.

From the Inside of Radical Wholeness: When Coherence Had to Carry Weight

I used to think coherence was something you returned to, perhaps like a meditative state, a place you could visit when life became too loud or too fast. Over time, that understanding changed, first in my own body, and then in the way I watched systems respond when pressure was real and unavoidable.

What I began to trust was not a feeling of calm, but a different kind of reliability. I could feel my system remain organized even as circumstances moved quickly, when decisions had consequences, or when relationships were strained. The difference was subtle but unmistakable.

In my life, coherence was less about comfort and more about integrity. Not moral integrity, but structural integrity, the kind that lets a system stay in relationship with what is happening without needing to distort itself to survive the contact.

Over time, this changed how I moved through my own life, and I began bringing less distortion into the spaces I entered. Coherence did not make things easy; it made participation more precise and relationships more honest, even when the outcomes were not simple.

When coherence cannot carry pressure, it is still a rehearsal. When it becomes durable, you live from it rather than return to it. It becomes the ground that holds you steady and the orientation that allows you to stay in contact without losing yourself in the process.

Chapter 11
When Wholeness Becomes Orientation

There comes a point in this work when coherence no longer feels like something you return to. It begins to feel like where you are standing. Not because life has become simple or because difficulty has disappeared, but because the system's internal organization has changed in a way that no longer requires continuous supervision.

The initial shifts are subtle initially, yet compound quickly and become unmistakable. You stop attending to self-correction. The energy you once used for monitoring, defending, and recalibrating becomes available for perception, for listening, for participation. Your whole system is no longer primarily occupied with creating boundaries against the world. You have enough internal coordination to meet what is here without fragmenting in response.

Earlier in the journey, you will experience coherence as a contrast to the old patterns. You notice relief where there used to be friction, and perhaps feel steadiness where reactivity used to take over. There might be more space in the body, with more room and a calmer cadence for the breath. Over time, even that contrast recedes—not because coherence has faded, but because it has become ordinary. The system no longer checks whether it is aligned. It moves from alignment because that is now how it is organized.

In biological terms, this is the difference between a system that must constantly correct for instability and one whose internal processes have synchronized enough that regulation becomes implicit. Information and energy can move without being scattered by internal interference. In a human life, this shows up as reliability: the capacity to remain intact amid complexity, to stay present in uncertainty, and to respond without having to first negotiate with oneself.

Life is still complex, and people are still unpredictable. Systems are still under strain. Even when the world doesn't change, a coherent system meets it differently. Wholeness begins to function less as a destination and more as the system's default condition.

This chapter follows the exploration of coherence under pressure for a reason. Pressure is where coherence proves itself. Orientation is what remains when that proof becomes lived reality.

By the time this shift became clear to me, coherence was already the ground of my work, my relationships, and my way of moving through the world. What changed was the architecture of my days. I remember realizing that I no longer had a "spiritual life," a "working life," and a "personal life" to align. Teaching, writing, listening, deciding, and resting were all happening from the same interior center. The coherence I had spent years learning to return to had become the place I was simply living from.

That was when orientation replaced effort. The work did not disappear, but it stopped feeling like a separate activity layered on top of life. Life was meeting me inside coherence, and coherence was meeting life with less friction.

The End of Self-Management

One of the invisible shifts in this stage is the gradual end of self-management as a central activity. Earlier phases of integration often require careful attention to triggers, patterns, timing, and internal somatic signals. That attentiveness is part of the apprenticeship; it is how the system learns to reorganize.

But eventually, coherence becomes stable enough that the system no longer needs to self-supervise to remain coherent.

Decisions begin to take shape with less internal negotiation. Attention no longer keeps looping back to check whether it is doing the right thing. Tone, posture, and impact start to arise from the system's organization rather than from strategies applied to it.

What this creates is availability. Energy that once went into monitoring becomes available for listening, for sensing the field of a situation, and for responding to what is present. And what enters through that availability is not just rest, but information. Somatic signals that were once drowned out by internal chatter begin to register with specificity. Clarity is available without internal argument, and insight feels as though it's received rather than manufactured, because the system is no longer distorting what it senses to secure itself against experience.

From a neurological perspective, this resembles the difference between a process that is tightly controlled from the top down and one that has been sufficiently integrated to operate through distributed coordination. The prefrontal cortex no longer needs to micromanage what the body and relational field have learned to do together. The system has reorganized to the point where coherence is maintained without constant oversight, even as it continues to refine and deepen.

This is also where my work with clients changed. When I sit with someone from a stable center, I am not trying to "fix" them or even encourage healing. I'm holding a field that can register more of what is true without flinching, and that alone tends to reorganize what becomes possible in the room. People feel it as safety, but more precisely, they feel it as permission: permission for their own system to stop negotiating with fear and start listening for their own truth.

Coherence as the Default Condition

As coherence stabilizes, it stops presenting itself as a state you enter and leave. It becomes the condition from which perception, timing, and response arise.

I felt this most clearly in the way my days began to arrange themselves. Halfway through a conversation or decision, I would realize I hadn't been managing my state at all. I had simply been present. The old habits of checking and preparing were still available, but they no longer ran the show. There was a quiet confidence in that: the sense that the system can meet what arrives without rushing ahead of itself.

This is not perfection. A day can still be tender. A moment can still land hard. But the system no longer spirals into self-attack or elaborate story. It returns more quickly because its default organization is intact. Repair becomes simpler, more like a recalibration than a collapse.

Over time, what once felt like work becomes the ordinary rhythm through which experience is metabolized and expressed.

The Ordinary Strength of Reliability

There is a temptation to treat late-stage coherence as a peak experience or a permanent calm. In practice, it is neither. It is simpler than that. It is more like gravity: always present, rarely noticed, structuring everything that moves.

It is not about how coherence feels, but how it functions. Attention is no longer consumed by protection or self-monitoring, so it can participate more fully in what is happening. Perception is less narrowed by threat or habit. There is a steady sense that what is needed can be sensed, received, and enacted without forcing.

Wholeness at this stage is not impressive, but dependable. You see it in how identity is not fazed by conflict, and how orientation remains dependable even in the face of uncertainty. Complexity no longer demands simplification to be tolerated. The human system remains itself while staying in relationship with what is unfolding and therefore can register more of what is happening rather than just what feels urgent or familiar.

This is functional integrity: a reliable way of meeting the world with the full bandwidth of perception and participation intact.

When Love, Creation, and Coherence Are No Longer Separate

Earlier in the human journey, Love, creativity, and coherence often appear as distinct capacities. Love feels like something you offer or protect. You summon or express creativity, and coherence is a quality you return to when things fall apart.

As orientation stabilizes, these begin to move as one integrated intelligence. Love becomes the organizing intelligence that allows perception to remain open. Creativity is the life-force that organically moves through what is perceived. Coherence is the structure that allows Love and creativity to happen without distortion or strain.

In this phase, Love, creativity, and coherence are no longer separate projects. They are one living process moving through different channels: perception staying open, energy staying in motion, and the whole system staying aligned enough for timing and intelligence to pass through cleanly.

Identity Without Vigilance

When our identity no longer needs to protect itself, something fundamental changes in how a person inhabits their life.

There is less effort spent maintaining a position and more continuity in how presence moves across situations. Personality does not disappear, nor does perspective. What falls away is the subtle labor of defending who you are in order to feel safe, acceptable, or intact.

One of the tender surprises for me was realizing how much energy had been going into protecting a version of myself I no longer needed to defend. I began to walk into rooms without pre-adjusting my tone, my story, or my position. I could let conversations unfold without quietly tracking how I was being perceived. That didn't make me less careful or less kind. It made me more available.

Neurologically, fewer resources are devoted to threat detection and self-correction, and more are available for perception, learning, and relational attunement. The system is no longer scanning for danger as its primary task. It is available for information, nuance, and timing.

In lived experience, this often feels like a quiet ease in being where you are. Attention stays with what is happening rather than looping back to maintain an image or position. The system stays in contact, and because of that consistency, it becomes more precise.

The Trust That Replaces Control

As coherence matures, trust begins to take the place of control—not as a belief about outcomes, but as confidence in the system's capacity to remain coherent as it evolves.

When there is less fragmentation in the system, experience can be met with more steadiness. Feedback is easier to receive without collapsing into shame or self-attack, and adjustment begins to feel more natural, more like responsiveness than failure. Because less energy is tied up in bracing for what might come next, more of the present can be taken in. From there, orientation becomes clearer, and participation less effortful.

In biological systems, this is how learning becomes sustainable. Coherent networks do not require a crisis to adapt. They adjust through ongoing feedback that the system can absorb without destabilizing core function. The same pattern appears here, not as a theory, but as lived capacity.

In practice, this feels less like managing life from the outside and more like staying present within it. Decisions no longer carry the same pressure to secure the future. Attention remains more available, less narrowed by defense. And when there is less inner noise, it becomes easier to recognize what is needed and respond with clarity. You can act decisively without needing to control life to feel safe in it.

Integrity as Living Coherence

At this stage, coherence is no longer something you practice in order to return to yourself. It is the way the system is organized.

Integrity becomes visible as structural honesty: the system's fidelity to coherence as its organizing principle, even as new material continues to arrive.

New material does not arrive as a disruption to eliminate. It arrives as information the system can include, reckon with, and reorganize within the whole. Another layer of memory or lineage pattern may surface, and coherence can meet it without treating it as regression. It becomes the next movement of the same intelligence that reorganized the system in the first place.

In complex systems, stability does not mean sameness. It means the capacity to reorganize without losing core function. Coherence is measured not by the absence of disturbance, but by the system's ability to absorb change without cascading failure. The same principle applies here. Integrity is not staying the same- it is staying coherent even while evolving.

This is where the Involutionary–Evolutionary Flywheel becomes self-sustaining. The system no longer cycles between breakdown and repair as separate modes. It continues to update itself through participation and reorganization without losing its internal coherence. Integration is not a remarkable event, but it is the way the system stays alive.

When I look back, what feels most significant is not that I became "better" at coherence, but that coherence no longer needed my supervision. It became the ground I stood on rather than something I had to keep rebuilding. The work didn't end, but it matured. It began to feel like life itself moving through a reliable instrument.

Orientation as a Way of Life

By this point, wholeness has become relational in its consequences. You experience a widening of care, a deepening of patience, and a steady capacity to remain in relationship with complexity without rushing to resolve it prematurely. You will have more space for listening and discernment, along with a growing sense that even unstable systems are carrying information that can guide what comes next.

Wholeness that has become orientation does not remain private, because coherence is never only an internal condition. It is relational and systemic. It changes the conditions under which interaction takes place, simply through presence without fragmentation.

At this point, having demonstrated the significance of coherent Beings, our question is no longer how a human being becomes whole. It is how coherence moves through families, communities, institutions, and cultures that are still organized around fragmentation, urgency, and fear. It is how coherence propagates, stabilizes fields, and alters collective dynamics simply by being present.

This is where Radical Wholeness leaves the domain of personal development and enters the domain of collective life.

From the Inside of Radical Wholeness: When Orientation Became Home

There was a long apprenticeship in my life where coherence was something I learned to return to. I trained myself to notice the subtle places I would split, rush, brace, or abandon my own deeper knowing, and I learned what it felt like to come back—over and over—until the return became trustworthy.

But at some point, the return stopped being the center of the story. Coherence became the place my life was already standing from. The energy that once went into monitoring became available for listening. The effort that once went into staying aligned softened into a steadiness I could rely on. And what moved in that steadiness was not only peace, but capacity: a wider bandwidth for truth, tenderness, intensity, complexity, and Love.

I began to feel what a coherent system brings into an environment, not as an idea, but as a condition. The field becomes more honest. What is true becomes easier to touch without dramatizing it or defending against it. In that sense, coherence becomes a form of service even before any words are spoken.

And this is where Love, creation, and coherence begin to behave like one intelligence. Love keeps perception open. Creation keeps life-force in motion. Coherence keeps the instrument aligned enough for timing and guidance to pass through cleanly.

This is what it means for wholeness to become a way of life. The work continues, because life continues. But the system no longer must fracture to participate. Orientation holds, and from inside that holding, life can finally meet you as you are: coherent enough to carry what is real, and open enough to let Love move.

Chapter 12
When Coherence Enters the Field

As coherence becomes orientation, it does not stay contained within a single nervous system. A coherent human system changes the conditions around it, often without trying. It shifts the pace at which information can be metabolized, the amount of truth that can be spoken without escalation, and the degree of complexity that can be held without collapsing into urgency.

We can name this spiritually, and many traditions do. You can also name it in the language of systems. In physics, coherence describes phase alignment, the kind of coordination that allows a signal to move without being shredded by interference. In biology, coherence across subsystems often determines whether stress becomes adaptation or breakdown. Human systems follow the same logic. When a field is organized by fear, speed, or status, it narrows its options and defaults to familiar loops. When coherence is present, more reality can be registered at once, and a wider range of responses becomes available.

This is why Radical Wholeness cannot end at personal integration. Fragmentation in our time is not only intrapsychic. It is ecological, cultural, ancestral, systemic. If wholeness is real, it becomes visible in what happens between us—how we hold contact, metabolize difference, repair, tell the truth, and move with uncertainty.

When coherence enters a field, the first change is often informational. A conversation that has been circling the same argument begins to sense the deeper question underneath it. A system trapped in false choices begins to perceive the unspoken options. The atmosphere can hold truth and tenderness in the same breath. It becomes easier for everyone in the field to consider what is being asked for.

I learned to notice this in the most ordinary circumstances: in conversations that used to tighten my body, in situations where urgency used to make everyone louder, in moments where the "right" move was less a strategy than a recognition. As coherence stabilized in me, I felt less compelled to manage the room. Instead, I would tend to the quality of presence I brought into it, and whether I could keep that frequency clear enough to stay in relationship with what was present.

Fields, Not Individuals

Modern materialist culture trains us to think in terms of individuals acting upon individuals. Living systems rarely behave that way. They function through fields: relational, informational, ecological, and cultural. Layers of conditions that shape what actions are available long before anyone decides what to do.

In physics, a field is a set of conditions that organizes how matter and energy interact. In biology, organisms are participants in nested ecosystems of feedback and exchange. Human systems are just fractals of this experience. Families, organizations, communities, and cultures develop default rhythms, thresholds, and "ways things go" that operate beneath our conscious intent.

When a coherent system enters an incoherent field, it does not override it. It introduces a different order into the shared space. In that presence, information can move with less distortion. Tension has more than one pathway. The field gains options.

This is rarely dramatic, but it is unmistakable. A group that has been locked in positional thinking becomes capable of naming the pattern it is caught in. Someone says what has been true for a long time, and the scenario can finally accept it. Or a stuck system recognizes its next step without being pushed. When that happens, it is usually not because a coherent person 'handled' the room, but because their steadiness reduced the noise enough for the field's own intelligence to become visible.

I have watched clients arrive convinced they need a better plan, when what they need is a field stable enough to tell the truth. When I stay coherent, the conversation stops performing competence and starts revealing reality. The turning point is often simple: a sentence that lands with quiet precision, and the shared exhale that follows, as if the system recognizes what it has known all along.

In group spaces, I've seen coherence shift a room without a single intervention. Someone speaks from a deeper layer than usual. Another person responds without defense. The pace softens. And suddenly, the group is no longer solving a problem; it is meeting a truth.

Coherence as a Stabilizing Attractor

In complex systems theory, an attractor is a stable pattern a system tends to return to, especially under stress. It doesn't dictate every outcome, but it shapes the default pathways: what the system repeats, what it reaches for, where it falls when uncertainty spikes.

Fear can function as an attractor, as can urgency or collapse. Many people know what it feels like to be snapped back into a familiar loop, even when their insight is real and their intentions are sincere. That snapback is not a moral failure. It is architecture. It is the system returning to the most available order it has.

One reason I teach Radical Wholeness as an inner architecture is that coherence is not maintained by willpower. As Parts are welcomed home and their protective assignments relax, the inner structure changes. Over time, coherence becomes less of a state you attempt and more of a resting place the system naturally returns to. Recovery becomes faster as the strain of returning becomes smaller. The organism can carry more life without breaking.

The same principle applies in shared space. In a fragmented field, small disturbances cascade quickly. Reaction becomes the fastest available coordination. In a coherent field, disturbance still occurs, but it doesn't seize the whole. Multiple response pathways remain accessible.

In physics, coherence helps preserve the clarity of a pattern or transmission even in the presence of noise. In living systems, when different parts work together, stress can be carried throughout the system without pushing it into collapse. In relational fields, coherence changes how quickly tension turns into threat, and how easily a system can return to contact.

A coherent human system can function as a stabilizing attractor in the spaces it enters—not by suppressing conflict or insisting on harmony, but by changing the conditions under which conflict spreads. Certain reactions lose momentum, and other patterns fail to lock in. Other forms of coordination become possible without being imposed.

You can feel this when a conversation that would normally collapse into blame stays oriented toward meaning. Or when a conflict that seemed irreconcilable becomes complex in the best way: both realities remain present, and a larger coherence appears that doesn't flatten either side. The system doesn't become "nice." It becomes more capable.

From Regulation to Resonance

Earlier stages of this work emphasize regulation because fragmented systems cannot participate in larger fields without first becoming internally organized. Regulation stabilizes the instrument. Resonance is what becomes possible when the instrument is stable enough to coordinate with life rather than defend against it.

Resonance is coordination without force. In neuroscience, it shows up when distributed networks synchronize without top-down control.

In ecology, it appears as self-organization around shared rhythms. In human groups, it emerges when people sync up in timing, when intelligence is not bottlenecked through hierarchy, and when people can feel what the field is asking for.

A coherent person does not manufacture resonance; they make it more available by staying whole and aligned. Less noise means more information can enter. It becomes easier to sense what belongs, what does not, and what is ready.

This does not require any supernatural claim. It happens when experience is not automatically processed through defense, and the system can stay in contact long enough for the full meaning to register.

There is an important ethical note here. I have been in spaces where words like "coherence" or "signal" were used to bypass accountability or cloak harm in spiritual language. That is not coherence. Coherence makes consequences easier to face because it reduces fog. It does not exempt anyone from repair.

Collective Systems Under Coherence

Families, organizations, and cultures don't change because people become morally better or emotionally smoother. They change when the conditions that sustain fragmentation are no longer the only available order.

In human systems, coherence often shows up as capacity: the capacity to face a truth without disintegrating, to grieve without collapsing into blame, to imagine without bypassing what is painful. A group discovers it can hold tension and meaning at the same time. The old choreography—withdrawal, attack, appeasement—may still be present, but it no longer dictates what must happen next.

The amount of intelligence the field can access in these coherent human systems is mind-blowing: widened perspective, less urgent timing, and more creative response become possible because the system is no longer trapped inside a single defensive loop.

In my own life, the proof wasn't that the conflict disappeared. The proof was that the conflict stopped deciding how I had to respond. I could stay in a relationship without abandoning or weaponizing my truth. That single shift changed what my relationships could metabolize.

The Ethics of Presence

At this stage, ethics is less about ideals and more about the order we introduce into shared space.

A fragmented system introduces distortion even when its intentions are good: urgency, defensiveness, misattunement, or the subtle pressure to resolve discomfort quickly. A coherent system introduces stability, timing, and relational clarity, even when the circumstances are difficult.

This is where a necessary safeguard belongs. Coherence does not exempt anyone from accountability. It does not dissolve bias, nor does it justify harm under the guise of "high vibration" or spiritual maturity. In fact, coherence tends to make accountability cleaner, because distortion becomes harder to hide behind. The more coherent the system, the more directly it can face what is true, repair what it breaks, and revise what it has misunderstood.

Ethical presence often looks simple: clarity without attack, truth that doesn't perform superiority, boundaries that don't require contempt, repair that doesn't demand self-erasure. A coherent presence does more than avoid harm. It makes a different quality of relationship available—one in which truth, timing, and care can coexist without being traded against each other.

Wholeness in Circulation

Radical Wholeness does not culminate in a perfected individual. It culminates in coherence in circulation.

When coherence is in circulation, it does more than stabilize what already exists. It makes new forms of relationship, creation, and collective response possible. A coherent human system becomes a point of transmission for forms of intelligence no longer confined to personal history, cultural habit, or inherited fear.

Radical Wholeness is a way that we create from the future: not as plans, but as possibilities that become speakable and livable because the field can finally hold them.

Wholeness moves through a world that is not yet whole by changing the conditions under which fragmentation can dominate. It does not conquer; it alters what can take root.

Closing Movement

Wholeness begins as healing, matures as orientation, and completes itself as participation in the intelligence of life.

Radical Wholeness is not a promise of a perfected person. It is the cultivation of a presence that can hold complexity without collapsing into urgency, remain in relationship without self-erasure, and meet change without becoming organized by fear.

In a world shaped by extraction, speed, and polarization, coherence is not a private luxury. It changes what can be perceived, imagined, and sustained. New futures do not take root because we argue for them, but because new orders become livable.

This is what it means for coherence to enter the field: not perfection, but participation. Not control, but a life no longer at war with itself. The point was never to become flawless. The point was to let Love hold the center strongly enough that something more truthful could move through.

A Closing Invitation

I don't know what pressures will shape your life or mine in the years ahead. I only know what I have seen to be true: coherence changes what becomes possible. It changes the kind of truth you can hold without splitting. It changes the kind of truth you can hold without splitting, what your relationships can metabolize, and what your work can serve.

If this book has given you anything, I hope it is not another demand to improve yourself. I hope it is permission—deep, embodied permission—to come home to yourself, again and again, until Love is not something you reach for, but the intelligence that quietly holds the center of your life.

Every act of wholeness changes the conditions around you: what your relationships can hold, what your work can serve, and what your presence makes possible in shared space. Over time, those small changes gather. They become a different kind of contribution—less a mission than the natural consequence of a life organized by Love.

If you wish to continue exploring this work, further writings and related resources are available at Living Portal and Living Portal Press.

www.LivingPortal.co

www.LivingPortalPress.com

Author's Note on Practice and Care

The CosmoSync Methods and the Living Portal framework are intended as educational and developmental tools. They are not a replacement for licensed medical, psychological, or psychiatric care. If you are experiencing acute distress, suicidal thoughts, psychosis, or trauma symptoms that exceed your capacity to stay grounded, please seek support from a qualified therapist, physician, crisis service, or emergency provider.

Radical Wholeness can complement clinical treatment, especially when practitioners are open to somatic, energetic, and Parts-based approaches. Engage these practices with discernment, and move at a pace that respects your nervous system. Love does not rush. Coherence unfolds in its own time.

If you are engaging in Parts Work within the Living Portal system, remember that Parts are approached here as sovereign inner Beings, and their pace matters. Practices such as creating a Mind Palace or other forms of inner architecture can support stability by offering a coherent inner landscape in which these Beings can rest, relate, and integrate. Move carefully, honor your capacity, and do not hesitate to seek support when needed.

Appendix A
A Brief Comparison of Parts- Oriented Frameworks

This appendix is offered for readers familiar with Parts-oriented therapies who want to understand how Radical Wholeness differs, not primarily in technique, but in ontology. The distinctions below are not critiques. Each framework named here contributed essential insights to the evolution of Parts work. Radical Wholeness arises from these lineages and moves beyond them by shifting the level of reality at which Parts, coherence, and healing are understood to occur.

What follows is a brief, orienting comparison.

Early Foundations: The Psyche as Multiple

Carl Jung

Jung was among the first to articulate the psyche as plural rather than singular. His work on complexes, archetypes, and the Self revealed that consciousness is inhabited by semi-autonomous inner figures, each animated by symbolic and archetypal energy. Jung understood these figures as orbiting a central Self and emerging through dreams, fantasies, and symptoms.

Jung's contribution was foundational: fragmentation was not pathology, but structure. Yet the psyche remained the primary container, and coherence was understood symbolically rather than as a relational or field condition.

Roberto Assagioli — *Psychosynthesis*

Assagioli extended Jung's insights into a developmental and spiritual framework. Subpersonalities were understood as expressions of a deeper Transpersonal or Higher Self, with healing framed as synthesis and ascent toward unity.

Psychosynthesis introduced an explicitly spiritual dimension to Parts work and emphasized will, purpose, and ethical maturation. However, its model remained largely vertical—oriented toward integration into a higher organizing center—rather than relational or field-based. Energetic language was present, but coherence was not articulated as a graded, multidimensional field condition.

Relational Turn: Compassion Over Control

Hal Stone & Sidra Stone — *Voice Dialogue*

Emerging in the 1970s, Voice Dialogue marked a significant shift. Rather than seeking synthesis, it emphasized relationships. Selves were given voice and agency. Awareness, not domination, created choice.

Voice Dialogue de-pathologized multiplicity, enabling individuals to differentiate between identity and internal states. Yet it intentionally avoided ontological claims. Coherence was understood as increased flexibility and awareness within consciousness, not as a systemic or field-level phenomenon.

Richard Schwartz — Internal Family Systems (IFS)

Developed in the 1980s and 1990s, IFS offered a clear and accessible architecture for multiplicity. Protectors, managers, firefighters, and exiles were reframed as benevolent sub-personalities organized around the principle of Self-leadership.

IFS powerfully normalized fragmentation as adaptive and made compassion central to healing. However, coherence remained internal to the psyche. The Self functioned as a psychological organizing center, and field, lineage, and energetic dimensions—when referenced—were not usually treated as primary organizing realities within the model.

Transpersonal and Systemic Expansions

In parallel with these developments, other lineages widened the frame.

- **Stanislav Grof** and **Christina Grof** revealed transpersonal, ancestral, and karmic dimensions of the psyche through non-ordinary states.
- **Bert Hellinger** demonstrated that Parts often carry systemic and ancestral loyalties.
- **Anna Wise** showed that coherence arises when diverse brainwave patterns synchronize.
- **Terri O'Fallon** articulated how awareness matures through distinct developmental perspectives.

Each of these contributions expanded *where* Parts could be located—across time, lineage, energy, and development. Yet Parts were still most often approached through the language of psyche, rather than as sovereign expressions of consciousness.

Contemporary Refinements Within the Psychological Paradigm

Steve March and other post-IFS innovators

More recent approaches have refined Parts work through trauma-informed care, attachment theory, and nervous system regulation. These contributions have increased safety, embodiment, and relational sensitivity.

They represent important methodological advances while largely remaining within the psychological paradigm. Parts remain internal psychological states to be regulated, integrated, or harmonized. Coherence is treated as a state to be achieved, rather than a field condition to be entered.

Radical Wholeness & Living Portal Parts Work (CosmoSync™ Methods)

Radical Wholeness arises as a threshold crossing in this lineage.

In the CosmoSync™ Methods, a Part is approached as an energetic intelligence—a holofractal expression of consciousness carrying memory across personal, ancestral, karmic, and collective dimensions. Coherence is not something the psyche achieves through management alone. It is understood here as a condition of relational alignment within a living field. Transformation occurs through resonance within a field of Love, not through analysis, control, or integration alone.

Parts are not absorbed into the Self. They engage in a relationship with it. Distinct waveforms synchronize without losing sovereignty. As coherence stabilizes, internal opposition softens, energetic waste decreases, and the system becomes capable of holding complexity without fragmentation.

Radical Wholeness does not replace earlier frameworks. It continues a trajectory they began by shifting the underlying ontology—from psychological organization to field-based coherence.

From this recognition, Living Portal Parts Work and the CosmoSync™ Methods emerged, not simply as reinterpretations of existing models, but through the development of practices designed to meet Parts as sovereign beings rather than sub-personalities.

Closing Orientation

What changes in Radical Wholeness is not only technique, but the level of reality at which healing is understood to occur. This ontological shift required the development of new relational and initiatory steps for reclaiming Parts as unique and sovereign energetic intelligences, capable of coherence beyond the psyche alone. Fragmentation is revealed not as failure, but as a phase within a larger process of reorganization. Coherence is not an achievement, but a lawful return to a more truthful and less costly order of being.

Appendix B
Overview of Parts Lineage & Frameworks

Dimension	Jung / Psychosynthesis	Voice Dialogue
What a Part Is	Complex / subpersonality	Sub-self/ inner voice
Primary Domain	Psyche (symbolic/imaginal)	Conscious awareness/ relational self-observation
Organizing Center	Self / Higher Self	Aware ego/ observing awareness
How Change Happens	Integration/ascent	Dialogue/differentiation
Role of Effort	Will and synthesis	Conscious choice and differentiation
Lineage & Time	Largely intrapsychic	Present- moment relational awareness
Energetics	Symbolic/subtle	Minimal or implicit
Goal of Practice	Unified or integrated selfhood	Flexibility and voice among selves
Typical Horizon	Symbolic integration/ vertical development	Relational differentiation without an explicit ontology

IFS	Contemporary Post-IFS & Trauma-Informed Parts Work	Radical Wholeness (CosmoSync™)
Psychological part or sub- personality	Psychological part shaped through attachment and somatic patterning	Sovereign energetic intelligence
Psyche	Psyche and nervous system	Field of consciousness across personal and transpersonal dimensions
Self	Regulated Self-presence	Coherence within a living field
Unburdening / Self-leadership	Regulation / relational safety	Resonance/entrainment/ re- synchronization
Compassionate Self-leadership	Regulation and pacing	Alignment rather than force
Personal biography	Personal biography and attachment history	Personal, ancestral, karmic, and collective
Present but not primary	Somatic/ physiological	Explicit and field-based and multidimensional
Internal harmony and Self-led relationship	Stability, safety, and regulation	Internal and Field coherence
Intra-psychic healing and harmony	Stabilization through safety and regulation	Participatory coherence and world-creative relationship

Appendix C
Glossary of Terms

Animate Paradigm

A way of understanding reality in which life is not inert, separate, or mechanical, but living, relational, and participatory. Within this paradigm, psyche, body, Earth, and cosmos are understood as expressions of one living continuum of intelligence.

Collective Field

The wider relational and transpersonal field in which individuals live is nested and through which they participate in larger patterns of coherence, fragmentation, memory, and becoming. It includes the individual but extends beyond the individual into ancestral, cultural, ecological, karmic, and quantum dimensions of shared reality.

Coherence

A lawful condition of alignment in which energy, information, and relationships can move through a human system with less internal interference. Coherence is not merely calm, regulation, or internal harmony, but a participatory condition of right relationship within a living field.

Coherence Chamber

A stable inner or relational environment in which fragmented Parts can be safely received, reorganized, and brought into harmonic relationship. It reduces overwhelm and supports the stabilization of a new inner order over time.

Cosmic Attunement

The fourth pillar of the Living Portal, through which creation is situated within a conscious relationship to Earth and cosmos as a living context. Here, the human being matures into more deliberate participation in a wider field of intelligence.

CosmoSync™

The integrated family of methods runs through all four pillars of the Living Portal. It is both a developmental path and an energetic technology through which Love organizes itself in human form.

CosmoSync™ Methods

The specific practices, sequences, and relational processes through which coherence is restored, stabilized, and extended across the four pillars of the Living Portal. These pillars are Radical Wholeness, Soul Alignment, WildCreator™, and Cosmic Attunement.

Devotion

The maturation of coherence into lived fidelity to what is true. Devotion is not sentiment or spiritual performance, but the way a life begins to organize itself when internal opposition has softened enough for Love to hold the center.

Entrainment

The process by which distinct Parts, systems, or waveforms come into harmonic relationship through resonance rather than force. In Radical Wholeness, Parts do not disappear into sameness; they synchronize without losing sovereignty.

Field-Based Coherence

An understanding of coherence as a graded condition of relational alignment within a living field, rather than merely an internal psychological state. This is one of the defining distinctions of Radical Wholeness.

Fragmentation

The condition in which aspects of the self or soul have become divided, cut off, or forced into conflict in order to survive. It is not a moral flaw but a costly organizational pattern in which life-force is bound up in protection and internal opposition.

Four Pillars
The four major movements of the Living Portal: Radical Wholeness, Soul Alignment, WildCreator™, and Cosmic Attunement. Together they form one harmonic continuum of becoming through which coherence is restored, directed, expressed, and widened into participation.

Inner Architecture
The intentional inner structure through which Parts can rest, relate, reorganize, and collaborate in a coherent way. Inner architecture gives form to coherence and helps the system sustain orientation under pressure and over time.

Involution
The inward movement of descent into memory, matter, lineage, density, and previously exiled experience in order to reclaim what has been split off, hidden, or held in rupture. Involution is not collapse, but retrieval.

Involutionary–Evolutionary Flywheel™
The repeating spiral through which consciousness turns inward to reclaim what has been fragmented, exiled, or densified, and then turns outward again to express recovered coherence as creativity, contribution, and participation. It names the rhythm of descent, restoration, and re-emergence that underlies the Living Portal.

Life-Force
The living energy of the human system that becomes bound up in fragmentation, protection, and interference, and that returns to circulation as coherence stabilizes. When life-force is restored, more energy becomes available for Love, perception, creativity, and participation.

Living Field

The larger animate field of consciousness and relationship within which healing, perception, and participation occur. The living field is not a backdrop, but the medium of life itself.

Living Portal

Not an identity or title, but a functional state in which coherence has become a person's primary orientation. A Living Portal is a human system through which perception, relationship, creativity, and Love can move with less distortion and greater fidelity.

Love

Not merely an emotion, virtue, or intention, but the living intelligence and organizing principle of reality. In this work, Love is the field through which coherence is restored, sustained, and expressed in form, and the guiding force that teaches us to move at the speed of Love: the pace at which wholeness, alignment, creative expression, and attunement can unfold without distortion.

Mind Palace

A specific form of inner architecture or coherence chamber in which sovereign inner Beings can rest, relate, reorganize, and collaborate. In this work, the Mind Palace is not merely symbolic or imaginal, but structurally supportive of coherence.

Ontological Shift

The movement from a psyche-bound, mechanistic worldview to an animate, relational, field-based understanding of reality. This shift changes not only how Parts are understood, but how healing, coherence, and participation are conceived.

Orientation

A stage in which coherence is no longer a temporary state one returns to, but the place from which life is lived. Orientation marks the maturation of wholeness into a dependable way of being.

Participation

The mode of living that becomes possible when a person is no longer primarily organized around fragmentation and self-management. Participation means living in a responsive relationship with life rather than standing outside it as an isolated Self trying to control or interpret it from a distance.

Parts

Distinct formations of consciousness are shaped around rupture, adaptation, protection, and continuity. In Radical Wholeness, Parts are understood not merely as psychological subpersonalities, but as intelligences that may carry personal, ancestral, karmic, and collective patterning.

Radical Wholeness

A field-based approach to healing and development in which fragmentation is restored into coherence through resonance, relationship, and Love rather than through management, control, or self-improvement alone. It is the first pillar of the Living Portal and includes the reclamation of Parts not only from wounds formed in this lifetime, but from deeper fractures carried across ancestral lines, karmic patterning, and the wider field of time-space.

Reclamation Across Time-Space

The movement by which Radical Wholeness restores Parts of the self that have been split off not only through present-life trauma, but through ancestral inheritance, karmic threads, and transpersonal patterning carried across time-space. It names one of the distinctive dimensions of becoming radically whole: gathering back what has been left in other layers of one's being so that coherence can be restored across dimensions.

Relational Field

The shared field of interaction in which Parts, people, and systems influence one another. Healing and development do not happen in isolation, but through relational conditions that allow resonance, trust, and reorganization to emerge.

Resonance
The harmonic correspondence through which Parts and systems begin to reorganize in a living field. In Radical Wholeness, resonance is one of the primary conditions by which coherence is restored without coercion.

Sequence of Coherence™
The natural progression through which what has been fragmented gradually returns to resonance, relationship, and lawful participation in a wider field of wholeness. It is not imposed from outside, but reflects the way living systems reorganize when interference begins to resolve.

Six A's
The six practical phases of Radical Wholeness: Acknowledge, Accept, Allow, Appreciate, Aspire, and Alchemize. These phases describe the spiral arc through which Parts are noticed, trusted, received, appreciated, reoriented, and transmuted.

Soul Alignment
The second pillar of the Living Portal, in which restored coherence becomes direction, orientation, and deeper alignment with one's design, purpose, and more truthful path of participation.

Sourced Creation
Creation that arises from coherence, Love, and deeper alignment rather than from fear, compensation, urgency, or self-proving. It becomes especially available through the WildCreator pillar once life-force has been reclaimed and stabilized.

Sovereign Inner Beings
The preferred Radical Wholeness framing for Parts when they are encountered not as subpersonalities to be managed, but as distinct intelligences with dignity, agency, and memory. These Beings can

return to the right relationship without losing their uniqueness or sovereignty.

WildCreator™
The third pillar of the Living Portal, in which recovered life-force becomes embodied creativity, contribution, and sourced expression. WildCreator names the liberation of creative force once coherence has made it safe to move.

Selected References and Influences

Parts Work and Psychological Lineage

Assagioli, R. (1965). *Psychosynthesis: A Manual of Principles and Techniques*. Hobbs, Dorman.

Jung, C. G. (1959). *Aion: Researches into the Phenomenology of the Self*. Princeton University Press.

Jung, C. G. (1968). *The Archetypes and the Collective Unconscious*. Princeton University Press.

Schwartz, R. C. (1995/2021). *Internal Family Systems Therapy* (2nd ed.). Guilford Press.

Stone, H., & Stone, S. (1989). *Embracing Our Selves: The Voice Dialogue Manual*. New World Library.

Transpersonal, Systemic, and Developmental Expansions

Grof, S. (2000). *Psychology of the Future: Lessons from Modern Consciousness Research*. SUNY Press.

Grof, S., & Grof, C. (1989). *Spiritual Emergency: When Personal Transformation Becomes a Crisis*. Tarcher.

Hellinger, B. (1998). *Love's Hidden Symmetry: What Makes Love Work in Relationships*. Zeig, Tucker & Theisen.

O'Fallon, T. (2006–present). STAGES model and related developmental teachings, referenced through published papers, public talks, and interviews.

Wise, A. (1996). *The High-Performance Mind: Mastering Brainwaves for Insight, Healing, and Creativity*. Tarcher/Putnam.

Consciousness, Neuroscience, and Coherence

Damasio, A. (1999). *The Feeling of What Happens: Body and Emotion in the Making of Consciousness*. Harcourt.

Friston, K. (2010). The free-energy principle: A unified brain theory? *Nature Reviews Neuroscience, 11*(2), 127–138.

McGilchrist, I. (2010). *The Master and His Emissary: The Divided Brain and the Making of the Western World*. Yale University Press.

Newberg, A., & d'Aquili, E. (2001). *Why God Won't Go Away: Brain Science and the Biology of Belief*. Ballantine Books.

Porges, S. W. (2011). *The Polyvagal Theory: Neurophysiological Foundations of Emotions, Attachment, Communication, and Self-Regulation*. W. W. Norton.

Siegel, D. J. (1999). *The Developing Mind*. Guilford Press.

Thompson, E. (2007). *Mind in Life: Biology, Phenomenology, and the Sciences of Mind*. Harvard University Press.

Thompson, E. (2015). *Waking, Dreaming, Being: Self and Consciousness in Neuroscience, Meditation, and Philosophy*. Columbia University Press.

Varela, F. J., Thompson, E., & Rosch, E. (1991). *The Embodied Mind: Cognitive Science and Human Experience*. MIT Press.

Developmental and Integrative Thought

Gebser, J. (1985). *The Ever-Present Origin* (N. Barstad & A. Mickunas, Trans.). Ohio University Press.

Graves, C. W. (1970). Levels of human existence. *Journal of Humanistic Psychology, 10*(2), 131–155.

Wilber, K. (2000). *Integral Psychology: Consciousness, Spirit, Psychology, Therapy*. Shambhala.

Animate Paradigm, Cosmology, and Living Systems

Bachelard, G. (1958). *The Poetics of Space*. Beacon Press.

Berry, T. (1999). *The Great Work: Our Way into the Future*. Bell Tower.

Berry, T., & Swimme, B. (1992). *The Universe Story*. HarperCollins.

Bohm, D. (1980). *Wholeness and the Implicate Order*. Routledge.

Capra, F. (1996). *The Web of Life: A New Scientific Understanding of Living Systems*. Anchor Books.

Kauffman, S. A. (1995). *At Home in the Universe: The Search for Laws of Self-Organization and Complexity*. Oxford University Press.

Lefferts, M. (2019). *Cosmometry: Exploring the HoloFractal Nature of the Cosmos*. Cosmometry Press.

Margulis, L., & Sagan, D. (1995). *What Is Life?* University of California Press.

Prigogine, I., & Stengers, I. (1984). *Order Out of Chaos: Man's New Dialogue with Nature*. Bantam Books.

Sheldrake, R. (1981). *A New Science of Life: The Hypothesis of Formative Causation*. Tarcher.

Teilhard de Chardin, P. (1955). *The Phenomenon of Man*. Harper & Brothers.

Mythic, Imaginal, and Cultural Frameworks

Campbell, J. (1949). *The Hero with a Thousand Faces*. Pantheon Books.

Eliade, M. (1958). *Rites and Symbols of Initiation*. Harper Torchbooks.

Hillman, J. (1975). *Re-Visioning Psychology*. Harper & Row.

Contemporary Public Influences

HeartMath Institute / McCraty, R. (1993–present). Research and public teachings on heart-brain coherence and related field effects, referenced through peer-reviewed and public-facing materials.

Schmachtenberger, D. (2020–present). Public lectures and essays on civilizational coherence, systems breakdown, and the "Third Attractor."

Sahtouris, E. (1998–present). Public talks and essays on symbiotic evolution and Gaia-informed cosmology.

Authorial and Proprietary Works

Woods, H. (2020). *The Golden Thread: Where to Find Purpose in the Stages of Your Life*. New Degree Press.

Woods, H. (2025). *Living Portal™ Initiation Curriculum, CosmoSync™ Methods, Sequence of Coherence™, and Involutionary–Evolutionary Flywheel™*.

Use of AI

Parts of this manuscript were developed in dialogue with AI language models, which were used to support idea exploration. All AI-generated content was reviewed, edited, and integrated by the author to ensure accuracy, coherence, and alignment with the intended meaning. The conceptual framing, structure, arguments, and all final editorial decisions are entirely the author's work, with AI serving as a creative and analytical tool—much like a research assistant or an editorial partner. Full responsibility for the content rests with the author.

9 781970 938005